D1104825

Solo and Sixty
in Costa Rica

by
Teresa M. Bevan

ISBN: 9798783128899

Typesetting and Cover Design
by John Vincent Palozzi

cover and interior pictures by Teresa M. Bevan

Published by
Bevan Press
bevanonmyown@att.net

Dedication

To the not-quite-ready-for-the-rocking chair "queenagers"
who dream it
and to the have-I-lost-my-mind ones
who dare to see it through.

"The only true voyage, the only bath in the Fountain of Youth, would be not to visit strange lands but to possess other eyes, to see the universe through the eyes of another, of a hundred others, to see the hundred universes that each of them sees, that each of them is."

Marcel Proust from *Remembrance of Things Past*, Volume 5, Chapter 2 of "The Prisoner," published in 1923

—

CONTENTS

INTRODUCTION

"What? Can't be." I did the math again and got the same number.

I punched the number of the coming year into my calculator and subtracted my birth year — again.

"No! I don't believe it, but, yes, I *will* be turning sixty!"

I folded over in my chair, head on my desk and moaned. My thirty-something office manager appeared from out of her office.

"T, what's wrong?" she asked.

"I'm OLD," I cried to her. "There're still so many things I haven't done!"

In four short months, I would turn the horrendous number of sixty years of age. Had I buried my head in the ground like an ostrich for the past year? Had I been living on a deserted island with no means of keeping time?

No. I had been living my life. My dull, boring existence. I woke up. I went to work. I went home. I watched TV. I went to bed.

Rinse and repeat.

I'd sworn in my earlier years, on Dylan Thomas' poem, that I would "not go gentle into that good night." I had vowed to go kicking and screaming, biting and cussing the whole way.

Yet, here I was, sedentarily watching the years tick off as fast as seconds on an egg timer. When you've been married eighteen years, divorced for decades, your children have moved away, and you live in a transient area where it's difficult to make and maintain friendships, it's easy to become a "Sleeping Beauty," lying around waiting for Prince Charming to bring you back to life.

Well, Prince Charming must have eaten the rest of that

poisoned apple because he hadn't shown up, and I knew I was on my own. You can sit around feeling sorry for yourself, blaming others around you, blaming men, blaming God, but it all comes down to YOU choosing not to let life sift through your fingers.

Something really special was called for, otherwise my birthday would arrive and find me horizontal with the covers pulled over my head in despair. It had to be stupendous. It had to be monumental. It had to be something I *really, really* wanted. And maybe in the process, I could get lucky. Wink, wink.

It was about time I started working on my bucket list.

My co-workers and acquaintances started throwing out ideas and suggestions.

"You should go on a singles cruise to the Virgin Islands," one tossed out.

Somehow the words single and virgin don't fit a soon-to-be sixty-year-old woman with three grown children.

I've never been on a cruise, but it just wasn't giving me that spark of adventure I was longing for.

"Oh, what about going to Las Vegas?" asked another.

Right. Let me lose my shirt as well as my youth.

I really didn't feel someplace in the U.S. was it either. I couldn't see any of their suggestions fulfilling my vision for a grand adventure.

Then, I remembered my virgin passport empty of stamps from far-away places, and I said to my co-workers, "I've never really left the United States before, except for that time I went with the ladies' church group to the Bahamas, but that hardly counts; you didn't even need a passport to go there.

"And I don't want to go someplace cold where I have to drag along a suitcase full of heavy clothes," further narrowing down the list of requirements.

The answer was beginning to take shape—someplace not too cold out of the U.S. where I can get a passport stamp. That stamp was crucial.

My boss's daughter had told me about her thriller vacation to Costa Rica where she zip lined through the canopy of the rainforest. I jumped out of my chair and shrieked, "Eureka, that's it!"

But, how am I gonna pay for it?

That's when you pray and bargain with God. "Lord, if this is to be, let me find a flight for under $300.00 and hotels for around $75.00 per night." And, damn, if He didn't deliver! The flight came in well under the goal I had set and every hotel met my price, plus they came with a picture-perfect postcard view and the friendliest of staff.

Why this prayer never works when asking for a man, I have no idea.

I chose not to participate in an arranged group tour. Instead, I found activities I wanted to do, mapped out where I wanted to stay in accordance with those activities, and then researched various modes of transportation to get there. Since I don't speak Spanish, I wrote down key phrases I might need on index cards and rehearsed them daily. I bought a pocketsize English/Spanish dictionary and downloaded a translator app onto my cell phone. Done. With all of this planning being done on my own, you would expect something major to go wrong. Well, it depends on what you call "major," but I learned a few things along the way.

However, I'm getting the coffee bean cart before the donkey because before I could leave, there were a thousand details to work out.

Once plans were solidly in place, I ran to my closet and dusted off my bathing suit. I tried on the suit to make sure it

11

would still stretch enough to encompass the circumference of my butt. One thing I hadn't planned for was the overgrown shrubbery sticking out of the bathing suit bottom.

As it does with many things in your later years, one grows weary of the battle. I had not donned a bathing suit in quite some time, so, since the forest wasn't disturbing any of the villagers, I let things slide. But with this birthday trip to Costa Rica approaching, I had to resolve this problem. I couldn't have the people of Costa Rica calling in sightings of a large, hairy bipedal hominoid zipping through the treetops of their rainforest.

Being single and sixty is like looking through a photo album of your youth; you see what you have done before and figure you're wiser now that you're older and what you attempted before will somehow work this time.

A few decades earlier, in post-divorce years, my friend, Jo, and I being the only divorced members of our circle of friends, were re-experiencing life as newly single women, me after eighteen years of marriage and Jo after twenty-three. "Get back out there," was the cheer yielded up from the pages of magazines and dating commercials, so we set about to do just that.

We threw out our granny panties and purchased our first thongs. This garment brought us back to the quandary of what to do about grooming "down there." Jo had the answer — waxing. It was what all the young women were doing, and it seemed like a plausible solution. No doubt by now, this process surely had been made efficient and painless.

We drove to a salon on Federal Highway and 163rd Street in North Miami Beach. Jo went first into the makeshift waxing area with partition walls that did not go all the way to the ceiling. I could hear most of the conversation between Jo and a heavily-accented Russian woman whom Jo had described as gentle and thorough.

12

Jo emerged, none the worse for wear, and now it's my turn.

Removing one's clothing in front of a complete stranger is odd at best, but laying down on a table and having said stranger position your legs like a frog being dissected in a laboratory is a completely different amphibian all together. She asked me in her heavy accent, "Joo vant Br-r-razilian like joo friend?"

I was unaware that wax jobs of your hoo-ha could come in a variety of styles similar to moustache options. Who knew? I assumed there was just one way to skin a cat and since Jo seemed pleased with her experience, I responded, "Sure!"

The wax was warm and quite exotic feeling as it was being spread down the right side of my labia majora (sounds like a South Asian fish entre at *Lemongrass*). The now intimate stranger gently patted on a gauze pad.

This isn't so bad after all.

The thought had barely finished forming in my brain when the gates of hell split open and inhuman guttural moans and demonic screams flooded the salon. They were coming from me. Tears blinded my vision as a string of obscenities fell from my lips while I looked down there expecting to see blood. I leaped off the table to start putting on my clothing, and the nice Russian lady who had just ripped hair out from its roots in my most sensitive lady parts tells me, "Joo can't go like dat! Joo must do dee utter side!"

THE OTHER SIDE? I had forgotten about the other side.

With tears streaming down my face and great wailing and gnashing of teeth, I dropped my drawers and climbed back upon the table. I braced myself against what I knew was coming and sobbed like an infant. I was to discover, this is the wrong thing to do as the tensing up of your muscles tells your capillaries that death is imminent and they explode out of sheer terror, leaving the most God-awful bruising that would bring an end to any boxing match.

Fast forward to preparing for the Costa Rica trip, I faced the mirror.

"Oh, hell, no! I'm not doing that again," I exclaimed as I stood there in my bathing suit. "Waxing is out!"

I dug through my bathroom vanity looking for my pink battery-operated trimmer/razor/ "weed whacker." Once I replaced the batteries, I set about addressing the problem.

With the shrubbery sufficiently trimmed, I moved on to the task of clothing selection. Bathing suit now packed, I purchased a Tilley adventure hat and Columbia quick-dry pants and shirts. Since baggage weight would be an issue on an international flight, I decided to forgo the rolling casket of a hard side suitcase in lieu of two colorful duffle bags. Everything I found for my trip was at a discounted price, but the most amazing find were my hiking boots. The most comfortable shoes I have ever put on my feet, and it's a good thing, too, since I was about to climb some unexpected mountains in my life.

Not only did Costa Rica leave pieces of itself in the tread of my shoes, but it left tracks on my soul as well.

DOWN THE RABBIT HOLE

"Ladies and gentlemen, welcome aboard JetBlue Flight #38 in route to Fort Lauderdale. Our flight time today will be two hours and thirty-five minutes. Please sit back and relax and give your full attention to our flight crew as they go over some important safety features," the captain drones over the intercom.

Do they still refer to those things as intercoms?

I close my eyes and whisper gratitude to God for such an incredible opportunity to visit Costa Rica. My mind wanders back to the first day of my journey a little over a week ago.

There's this guy. *He* smelled so fresh and clean; not like the two fermenting elderly men sitting next to me on this flight, marinating in "Ode de Old Man" after shave. I brush aside the assault on my senses and drift off to my thoughts of *him*.

I'm experiencing an odd mixture of emotions as I pass through airport security to find my departure gate. Sort of a nervous peaceful anxiety. My first time heading out of the United States of America. I had traveled to the Bahamas with a group of church ladies, but that hardly counted since I didn't get a stamp on my passport. Hell, I didn't even *need* a passport on that trip. A *real* travel experience involves adventure, suspense, romance, and a freaking stamp on your passport!

And I am going solo.

I push my way through the crowded airport and plop down in the only empty seat available at the terminal gate. I look up at the bearded man seated across from me.

Terrorist! The thought reverberates against the insides of my skull.

Hold up there, girl, I say trying to snap my brain back to

15

reality. *Just relax.* While it's true that international travel is somewhat sketchy these days, it's not like I'm traveling to, say, Detroit.

The bearded young man I had so abruptly tagged a terrorist, sports a dark reddish-tone full beard. Albeit nicely groomed, it is very thick and not unlike the ones seen in photographs of, well, you know, *terrorists.* Looking past the beard, I notice the piercings, one in his left eyebrow and several in the earlobes.

Do terrorists do piercings? He's wearing a black knit skullcap under the hood of a white and black hoodie, with the Marvel Comic *Punisher* skull on the front. His washed out jeans have the appropriate raveling tears, and he has on clean, white untied hiking boots and earbuds in his ears listening to something on his phone. He kept his head down until feeling my gaze burning holes into his skull…err, the one in his head not the one on his shirt. He looks me straight in the eye. I flash an, "Oops! He caught me staring," grin. He returns a, "Caught you looking," smile.

"Ladies and gentlemen, we would like to invite passengers seated in rows fifteen to twenty to now board the aircraft."

I leap toward the line of passengers, jumping in ahead of the others, anxious to find a space in the overhead compartment for my carry on. Yeah, I'm one of *those* people. We stop at yet another security checkpoint entering the gangway then pass on following the line of passengers. The procession comes to a grinding halt down the narrow corridor, and I hear someone walk up behind me.

It would be rude of me not to say "hi," I thought. *Besides,* I scolded myself, *didn't you promise to crack open that shell you've been living in to reach out and meet new people on this trip?*

I turn and say, "So, are you going on vacation or are you going home?"

It was him! *How did he get up behind me? I thought I had left him in the dust back at the gate.*

"Going home," he says, smiling a big grin behind the beard, "and you?"

I wonder if the TSA missed some disguised explosive or deadly box cutter he might be carrying.

"I'm heading out to an adventure in Costa Rica," I say, trying to open up the translator app on my phone.

Our conversation is put on hold as we file onto the plane, doing a death-row shuffle as the passengers ahead of me clog up the aisle. We come to a complete stop.

Come on, move out of the aisle. And don't go taking up the space above my seat, either, all the while, being ever so conscience of the terrorist behind me.

Is he looking at my butt?

The aisle narrows again just past Preferred Seating. *If this gets any narrower, I'll have to inhale my thighs.*

I check my boarding pass again to make sure of my row and drop my carryon in the aisle seat of row 18. I swing the backpack off my shoulder, almost clipping some guy in the seat in front of me.

You're doing the same crap the other passengers are doing. Move out of the aisle, Teresa. I grab up the carryon and try to hoist it over my head into the overhead, but my terrorist acquaintance takes it from me and effortlessly shoves the bag into the compartment.

"Thank you," I say.

I sit down in seat D on the aisle, and look up to see him putting his bag in the compartment next to mine.

The nerve of him to put his bag next to mine before he reaches his seat!

17

Then he just stood there next to me. *Oh, God, I've picked up a stalker!* I feel a surge of panic as old episodes of *Criminal Minds* flash through my brain.

"Oh!" I say out loud but thinking to myself, *surely, he must be taking someone else's seat.* It must have shown on my face, because he holds out his boarding pass with his seat assignment 18E.

"I'm Jon," he said, offering his hand.

"Teresa."

To survive the shrinking of my personal space from claustrophobia, I normally have to down a Xanax or two — okay, four, but only once when I was in the middle seat. Don't judge me, please.

However, Jon keeps me so distracted with his charismatic personality and engaging conversation in spotty English that I barely notice the plane taking off.

If he has a box cutter, you're gonna die first, or maybe he'll use you as a hostage or human shield.

As the flight continues southward, the heat rises in more ways than one. I take off my sweater; he wrestles to remove his sweatshirt, almost removing his t-shirt, exposing several tattoos in the process...and those biceps. My ears pop and so do my eyes.

Stop noticing his muscles! He's probably your son's age. Yes, but he's NOT your son, now is he? Responded the little red devil on the opposite shoulder.

"What does this say?" I ask, gingerly running my finger over the upper portion of his left arm trying not to appear too obvious.

Stop it. Control yourself. Oh, man, his skin is soft. Have you lost your mind? He's just a boy!

He pulls up his sleeve further (*gulp*) to expose the remainder of the tattoo, and says, "It's Psalm 23 in Hebrew. My grandmother used to say to me every night before I go to bed. This one over here," he says, pulling up his other sleeve (*wow*), "is African. Means warrior, a strong protector. Up here is John 3:16, and the one on my back is a cross." He twists in his seat to expose his upper back. (*Dear God*)

"Mm, My son has a cross on his upper arm," I say, half in conversation and the other half in reminding myself that he probably *really* is the age of my son.

"How old is your son?" he asks.

Oh, God, he had to ask that question, didn't he? LIE, you idiot, LIE!

I told him my son's age, and he told me his.

Twenty-seven.

There, you see, he's older than your son. No, he's your daughter's age. Now, you're stealing your daughter's potential boyfriends. She's not here. What is wrong with you?

The Battle of Good vs. Evil continues to rage in my mind as we talk about family and share pictures. He shows me photos through a broken screen on his phone of his dog, named…something-or-other—*I suppose I should be listening.* I see him as a police officer without the beard in Costa Rica—*Ooo, this man in a tight uniform.* He's in a photo visiting Ground Zero in New York City showing the progression of the beard—*I prefer him with the beard.* There are some selfies of him in the bathroom mirror, which he swipes over much too quickly, but I manage to keep my mouth under control—brain not so much.

"I…I have two cats, and here are my kids," I reciprocate with pictures; partially hoping the action will snap my hormones back to post-menopausal levels.

"What do you do?" he asked.

"I work for financial advisors."

"No, I mean, what do you do for fun?"

19

Fun? I had to stop and think. Up until now, fun wasn't something I gave much thought to. *I could have some fun with you. Stifle yourself.*

"I've been hitting the gym in preparation for this trip," trying to make it sound like I enjoy it.

"I love the gym!"

No shit.

"What else?" he asked.

"Ummm, I like to go to the range for target practice."

"No way!" His green eyes widening as he leans forward in his seat. "You like to shoot? I show you the gun I want." He pulls up a picture on his phone.

You show me yours, I'll show you mine.

"Aww, that's nice one," Jon says after we exchange firearm photos. I show him shots of my finished targets, and we are both impressed.

"I try to join the French Foreign Legion, but there was some problem with my eyes..."

Those gorgeous sea-glass green eyes. Pay attention!

I think the Foreign Legion sounds a bit far-fetched, and it shakes me out of my delirium momentarily until he shows me photos of himself and a friend in front of the Legion building in France.

"Where are you going in Costa Rica?" he asked.

Anyplace you take me, sweet thang. Focus.

"Once I land in San Jose, a driver from the hotel in Alajuela will pick me up. Tomorrow morning, I'll take the bus north to La Fortuna. Two days later, I 'll take a boat across Lake Arenal to Monteverde"

As I answer with the locations on my itinerary, he draws a map on his thigh of the places I will be visiting. His knee is Nicaragua.

20

"Here. Here is my hometown," and shows me his hometown of San Ramon, close to Alajuela.

Hummm, maybe I should lie and say I'm going to the border of Panama.

At this point, I'm thinking I've got Tourette's Syndrome the way my brain keeps snapping back and forth and I can't seem to control my eyes.

Am I that starved for affection that I would seduce this… child? I haven't been attracted to any man for years, but this is irrational. Am I just desperate? It's absurd to be attracted to a man so young. Have all my dates been with younger men? I drift off to consider this question.

After my divorce decades ago, there was absolutely no interest in men or dating. My focus was strictly on my relationship with God and raising my three children. Then a year later, I became interested in a man I worked with even though he was much younger. We had a fabulous connection on the phone for about a year before we finally met. The age difference was never an issue, or so I thought. Five years later, after planning for marriage and the future, he ghosted me.

Nothing says "I love you" like a man who just drops off the planet. I experienced two more relationships like that throughout the years; marriage planning, then the David Copperfield routine. Two of them gave me coffee makers. Maybe that's an instinctual throwback equivalent to an ancient dowry of five shekels and a goat.

Following the ectoplasmic apparitions, I took everyone's advice that said: "Go online." And so I did. I clicked on the Internet to find love.

Nothing says "you're pond scum" like online dating. You're judged on your measurements and how closely you can imitate a frog: how fast you can hop into bed with a complete stranger and then hop onto another victim.

ONLINE DATING

Jon turns to the man seated on his right and begins a conversation in Spanish, giving me the opportunity to reflect upon the hot lust which threatens to consume my logical thinking like ravenous red-bellied piranha on a hapless heron.

Would I have been so attracted to him had I seen his profile on the Internet instead of in person? Probably not since the algorithms set up on dating websites like these usually prevent you from seeing potential dates that are not within your age bracket, even though younger men have found their way around it in the past. If I were to see Jon online, I would have moved on without contacting him because of his age, as I have done with the others.

But, this isn't online. He's right here. Close enough to touch.

Show me those tats again, Sugar.

I sneak a peek at Jon. He's still conversing with his neighbor. I slide my arm closer to his on the armrest. He doesn't move away.

Resistance to temptation is much easier from the other side of the proverbial looking glass than when it's rubbing elbows with you on a plane.

This pause for reflection back into my online experiences revealed two interesting truths—well, three if you count the coffee makers.

One, I am routinely attracted to men who are approximately ten years younger than myself.

Two, they are all homeless in some fashion. They either lived with their mothers or they had a roommate, but none had an actual apartment or house to call their own.

Whadya bet Jon lives with his mother?

Mentally, I begin running through my online experiences like flipping through an old card catalog in a library. That was my generation's Google.

My first online date was with a decent looking guy who claimed to be an actuary. I confess I had to look this term up before I knew what it meant. Something to do with math. I hate math, but as long as he didn't expect me to participate in some sort of math sex game, I'd cope. His online photos showed an attractive, well kempt man. On the phone, he was pleasant, intelligent, and seemed quite normal.

We agreed to meet at my favorite location on Key Biscayne, Florida, a perfect spot on the water with a stunning view of the Miami skyline. Out back, there is a lovely seating area, where on a cool evening, you can enjoy a glass of chardonnay by a roaring fire pit.

I arrived and waited outside by the fire with my wine.

And I waited, and waited, and waited some more to the point where the flames shooting out of my eyes were more sinister than those rising out of the fire pit. My phone finally rang as I exited the bathroom on my way to the car.

"Where are you?" I said, my words sizzling like the moisture boiling out the logs in the fire.

"I'm sorry, but the bus didn't come, and I had to walk." He was out of breath.

"You don't own a car?"

"Not yet. I told you I had just moved back to the United States and haven't had time to purchase one yet," he said.

Since it sounded plausible, I asked, "So, where are you now?"

"I'm on the mainland. Would you consider coming my way and we'll find a new location to have dinner?"

I know the area because my aunt and uncle live just off US Hwy1, so I suggest a restaurant nearby. I agree to meet him, making numerous cautionary remarks about not standing me up again.

It's a short drive across the causeway to the other restaurant. I chose a tiny bistro with low, romantic lighting and appealing smells emanating from the kitchen. No one is waiting outside, so I go in. The waiter shows me to a table for two, and I sit down with my back to the door. Still no one, so I order a drink. I called him, "Where are you?"

"I'm almost there," he replied, huffing and puffing like an emphysema patient climbing a mountain.

A man dressed in a jogging suit approaches from behind me and slides into the seat across from me at the table.

"I am so very sorry to have made you wait." He apologizes as the waiter arrives. I order dinner, since by now I'm starving, then the waiter turns to him.

"Oh, nothing for me, thank you, I'm not really hungry. Just coffee."

My eyes narrow with swelling suspicion, as my vision adjusts to the low light. I notice he isn't wearing a shirt under the 80's-style jacket of his electric-blue jogging suit. I knew his hair was red from his online profile, but here in its current state of fuzzy disarray, he resembles Bozo the clown. Then, I see his dirt-encrusted fingernails. The cuffs of his jacket were both dirty and frayed, much like his nerves. His movements are short and jerky, and he reminds me of a squirrel trying to cross a busy highway.

Should I have jumped up and left the restaurant? Of course I should have, but it's in the "should have" section of my life where I always screw up. I ignore flapping red flags in my brain trying to catch my attention as to say, "RUN, FOOL."

Throughout dinner and a piece of dessert split in half, we

25

have a flowing conversation, but those red flags keep popping up on specifics of his life's story.

"My girlfriend and I broke up while we were living in Puerto Rico," he said, "and she took all of my things, including my daughter. The job situation was very poor for actuaries there, so I decided to come back to the U.S."

Red flag. During initial conversations, he said this took place in Panama.

"I contacted a friend of mine whose daughter I tutored in math and she is letting me sleep on her couch until I can find a job."

Red Flag. He doesn't have a car or an apartment. Not even a hotel?

Eventually, the waiter comes to tell us they are closing and wish us to pay the bill. Basically saying "get the hell out." Since HE asked me out on this date, I assumed he would take care of the check. What is that old adage? "If you assume, you make an ass out of u and me." I excuse myself and leave for the bathroom in preparation for the forty-minute drive back home.

When I return, he is standing in the foyer surrounded by the servers and the manager.

"What's going on?" I asked.

"Uh...uh...well...I'm a little short on cash. Since I was walking, I didn't have time to stop at an ATM," he stammered. Red flag.

Should I have left his ass there to be arrested by the police for not paying the bill? Of course I should have, but instead, I pull a twenty-dollar bill from my wallet, and say, "How short are you?"

An actuary who can't pay a dinner bill?

"$8.00," he said. I hand him the twenty and walk outside, disgusted...with myself for being so gullible. He meets me outside, still apologizing, and it's then that I see by the glow of the streetlight the rest of his appearance.

His matching electric-blue polyester jogging pants with the white stripes down the sides are several inches too short, exposing his ankles. The sneakers aren't his because the toe box of the shoes are cut out to make room for his toes that hang over the end of the shoes by a good inch. His grimy hands are clutching what I presume to be all his worldly possessions in a beat up, dirty backpack.

I'm on a date with a homeless man!

He resigns himself to the fact that the evening is over (duh), but asks if I can drop him off at the house where he is staying.

Should I have said NO? Of course I should have, but instead, I agree to drive him.

There ya go being gullible again. When is this gonna stop with you?

Up until now, the flavorful smells from the restaurant and the outdoor breezes had been my friends, because once inside the closed container of my car I got a whiff of him. The smell is somewhere along the lines of a gym sock pulled from a sewer then discarded in a dumpster full of half-empty sardine cans left out to marinate during a Miami summer.

With my window down—he wanted his up because he was cold...*well, no wonder, you're not wearing a shirt*—I drive as fast as I can following his directions.

He has taken me around so many corners that I am now lost.

I finally pass the point of fear that he's gonna stab me to death with a knife that he probably stole from the restaurant. I open my mouth to say "ENOUGH!" when he points and says, "There, that's the house right there." I slam on the brakes.

He opens the car door, then turns to look at me. "Would you like to come in?"

Is he out of his mind? I answered with a stentorian, "NO." The fear is back, and I visualize him breaking into this house where he probably murdered and dismembered the owner earlier in the day, then buried her in a shallow grave out back. That would explain his tardiness and the dirt under his fingernails.

He left my car without further adieu and walked towards the house…along with the change from my twenty-dollar bill.

Months later, he sent me an email letting me know that he had been a "guest" of the Miami-Dade Police Department, arrested for vagrancy and was given a free "vacation" out of town, bound for Texas. I should learn to trust my instincts.

Were there other homeless characters I've attracted online? Well, I've gotten an offer from a ginormous bald man wearing only a Speedo and tattooed face to toe and a man wearing a dead beaver on his head—yes, I said a dead beaver. This guy was a Native Indian reenactment performer who lived in a tent. I like camping, but there was no way I was sleeping with that beaver. I hear they bite. There was the Canadian badminton player, the eighteen-year old who asked if he could call me "Mommy" if we had sex, and the man who proudly advertised himself as an available cuckold. Then there was "Capt. Morgan." I met the Captain at Dunkin Donuts where he didn't buy me a drink and talked only about himself, before standing up, putting his foot up on the bench upon which I was seated, struck the Capt. Morgan pose thrusting his genital area in my face and said, "Well, what do ya think?"

These and the numerous others who just cut to the chase and simply sent me photos of their private parts, which weren't distinctive enough to merit a mention, are the reasons I've hung up my mouse to online dating.

PURA VIDA!

Thrusting the image of Capt. Morgan out of my mind, I turn to look at Jon.

My God, what an improvement over my online experiences! He has stopped talking to the man on his right and is smiling at me as he runs his right hand through his thick, wavy black hair.

"Tell me about your parents, Jon," in a cheap attempt to psychoanalyze him. Not that I'm trained in this, you understand. It's all those *Criminal Minds* episodes.

"Well, my mother left me with my grandmother when I was a baby and I haven't seen her since, and my father lives away with his new wife."

Ah, mommy issues.

We lean in closely to be heard above the noise in the plane, not wanting to miss a single word the other has to say. I can feel the heat radiating from his face onto my cheek and wafts of his fresh scent lingers in my sinuses. Communication is going so well with the use of hand gestures, my pocket-sized English/Spanish dictionary, and a small assistance from the translator app on my phone that the conversation feels seamless.

"Are you going back to Costa Rica to visit your family?" I asked poking for information with my dental pick.

Please don't be homeless.

"Yes, I need to, umm, get my head on straight. I lost everything to a business partner who stole from me." He became quiet at this point and the conversation stopped as his clear green eyes glaze over in sadness. After a few moments, he says, "*pura vida*, life goes on."

I've read about the intentions of this expression in the Costa Rica culture before the trip. It means "pure life" or "simple life," so I understand his use of it, but I can't resist watching him grope to put things into English, as his shoulders scrunch up to his ears and his hands turn out with lack of words, so I pretend not to know what it means.

He is so cute, I just want to stroke that beard and kiss down the side of his tattooed neck.

Focus on the conversation!

Bring me those luscious lips, you gorgeous thing. WHAM! My voice of reason just took my impetuous nature to the wrestling mat.

"The air in my country smells so clean and fresh," Jon says inhaling deeply.

If it smells anything like you, I'll be in heaven. BLAM! Impetuous wraps its legs around the neck of my voice of reason in a "hurricanrana" wrestling move and squeezes.

"I know you are going to love it," Jon says practically bouncing with excitement. His love for Costa Rica is palpable as he goes on to describe its lush foliage, the fresh air, the flowers, and the beaches.

Then came the second question I've been dreading. "How old are you?"

Clenching my hands together and shifting in my seat, I tell him, "Sixty."

"NO! You sixty? NO," he exclaimed smacking himself on the forehead, which coincidentally is the same thing happening to my brain right now.

I show him my passport and again he scoffs, "NO! You so alive! Your face shows *pura vida*! Your eyes...can you take off your glasses and let me see your eyes?"

I remove my glasses and he stares deeply into my eyes, just inches from my nose.

Yeah, baby.

"NO. You have life in your eyes. Forty, I think," he says.

Feigned or otherwise, it matters not to me. I am sucking up his flattery faster than an alcoholic at an open-bar wedding. I don't care if he is a terrorist.

"Age means nothing in Costa Rica," he said. "If you have life…that's what matters. You know, my last girlfriend was fifty."

DING! DING! DING!! YES, we have a winner!! My hypothalamus has its hands raised in victory and its foot up on the gray matter of my prefrontal cortex in complete domination.

Desperately trying to maintain some form of decorum, I say, shifting away from that topic, "I wanted to go to Limon to see the orphaned sloth sanctuary, but I couldn't fit that into this trip."

Jon frowns, "Limon, is not so good right now. Listen. Listen to me. When you are out, put down your phone. Pay attention. Look around. See what is around you. Many thieves in Costa Rica. Here are my cell and home phone numbers. You call me and I will drive you anywhere you need to go."

Oh, Glory. He's not homeless and he has a car.

"You should not go to the bus stop in San Jose. It is in a not so good part of town. Use the bus station in San Ramon. Is much safer," he said, "and maybe you will go to dinner with me one night?"

WHAT WAS THAT? Did he just say that for real or did I imagine it?

No voice of reason could *begin* to talk me out of my obsession this time.

"Yes, I would love that!"

"Are you a citizen or a visitor," said the flight attendant suddenly standing next to me passing out some kind of paper. In dazed incredulity, I tumble the question around in my brain. *Is he asking if I'm a citizen of the U.S. or a citizen of Costa Rica? Wasn't I just having a romantic dinner with Jon? Where am I?*

"¿Es usted un ciudadano o un visitante?" said the flight attendant, shaking a piece of paper in my face.

Jon leans over and answers the attendant for me in Spanish.

"What is this?" I ask Jon, shaking the piece of paper.

"It's for Immigration," he told me, "I help you."

We muddle through the form; his hand brushes against mine and lingers a bit longer than necessary.

We deplane — *is that a word?* — in San Jose. The passengers push us along the gangway and Jon and I become separated. I stop and stand against the wall to wait for him. As he comes around the corner, he breaks into a huge smile as our eyes meet. He grabs my elbow to steer me along the hallways, winding towards Immigration and Customs.

The hallway ends in a large open area that splits us into two groups: citizens and visitors. I quickly realize his citizen line is going to take much less time than my visitor line, but there is no way to tell him to wait for me as I watch him get swallowed up by the crowd.

Well, that's that then. He'll just go on his way without me. It's for the best. He's way too young to be jumping his bones, anyway. Besides, I'd probably throw my back out.

I shake my head to free myself from the lustful trance I've been under as I wait in line. I survey my surroundings and look behind me at the two-story floor-to-ceiling glass wall I missed on my way in. .

"Oh My God!" I let out a gasp. "That's incredible!" I turn to the person behind me, "Look, it's a volcano. It's a freaking volcano!"

Either the person didn't speak plain insanity or they were deaf, but they neither turned to look nor did they respond, but just kept looking forward with a deadpan stare.

34

Humph, they must be from New York. They know how to ignore crazy there.

Every shade of green in the Prismacolor pencil box of one hundred and fifty colors jumped through the window to greet me. Deep forest green and hunter green of pines, the dark matte color of shamrock, vibrant lime green of new growth in spring, emerald greens so intense they sparkle like the jewel in the sunlight, and the seafoam green of paradise. There are blends of yellow and green like pears, the antique green of gray and brown of olives, and the washed out tones of green and grey in sage, all coming together for a buffet of hues in a feast for the eyes. Jon wasn't exaggerating when he described the greens of Costa Rica.

At the front of the visitor line, I'm directed to one of the five booths of immigration agents.

Oh, my God, this is it. This is where I get my stamp!

Ninety percent of my choice to make this journey to Costa Rica was to get a stamp on my virgin passport, and now it's here. I pranced like a Lipizzaner stallion.

Security motions me forward to the booth. I slowed my prance. Not everyone likes a parade.

"Hola!" I greet the woman behind the Plexiglass. "I don't know what to do. This is the first time I've ever left the United States with the exception of the Bahamas, but that really didn't count since I didn't even need a passport. This is my birthday gift to myself. What should I do?" *Don't forget to breathe.*

She checks the date on my documents.

"Happy birthday," she says with the slight grin of an agent instructed to look forbidding. She picks up a large stamp with a wooden handle and slams it down onto a page in my passport creating my very first stamp.

"IT'S NO LONGER A VIRGIN!" I squeal out loud, throwing my arms in the air like I'm Jerry Rice making a freakin'

35

touchdown. Obviously not the normal behavior in Immigration since no one joins me in celebration and no applause spontaneously erupts.

Another agent waves me on.

Is that it? Is that all I get? No rum-filled pineapple drink with a little umbrella as a "Welcome to Costa Rica" pleasantry?

I follow the crowd toward the left. In the next room, Jon stands waiting for me in all his Tico lusciousness.

Stop it, you cradle robber.

Shut your mouth, she's allowed a vacation fling if she wants.

He has mommy issues. Leave him alone.

Bite me!

"What now?" I ask Jon as he grabs my elbow again and moves me through the terminal.

"Baggage."

According to many online blogs, lost luggage could be the norm, but there it is, my duffle bag with a pattern that looks like Jackson Pollack's splatter painting, "Constant Change," all in one piece and practically glowing on the conveyor belt.

Jon snatches my bag along with my carryon.

Big, moist brownie points for being a gentleman.

"No, let me," I said, "I better get used to lugging these things around on my own since that's what will be happening for the next eight days." Reluctantly, he hands over the bag.

In the next room, several lines form for the final checkpoint before leaving the airport. Jon stops dead in his tracks.

"What's wrong?" I asked. But his intense gaze focuses upon the Customs agents, first one then another. Lanes, established using those movie theater ropes, divided the crowd into six lines. Jon grabs my elbow and steers me from one line to the next, saying only, "I can't go through here." Travelers begin stacking up behind us until I get caught up in the swell of people and swept toward an agent.

I hand my passport and immigration paper that I had filled out on the plane to the inspector, and plop my bags onto the conveyor belt. They disappear through the x-ray machine, and security waves me to the left where they wand me.

That could sound kinky, but not with this old sour puss.

I collect my things on the other side and look around for Jon just in time to see him on the *right* side of the x-ray machine digging through his bag with the Customs agent. They finish digging and the agent sends him on, but not through the metal detectors or x-ray machine. He didn't even get wanded.

Now it sounds kinky, but why did he get a pass?

Jon gathers his bag and escorts me toward the exit.

"What...why..." The pushing of the crowd and the noise keep me from forming a coherent sentence.

The exit is comprised of two regular size glass doors through which the whole of Costa Rica travelers had to pass to get out of the terminal. The horde sweeps us out the doors to the smell of exhaust. A throng of men with signs pressed up against a Plexiglas wall to my right shout out names of travelers they've come to collect.

"What's your name again?" Jon yells above the cacophony of drivers, planes, and horns.

He doesn't remember my name?

"Teresa! My name is Teresa," I shout back.

I keep looking for my driver. The hotel had arranged for a man named Carlos to meet me at the airport and drive me to my hotel.

How many men named "Carlos" could there be in Costa Rica?

My Carlos' phone number is buried in my bag, but the crowd is moving so quickly, I don't have time to stop and search

37

for it.

"If you don't see your name, I will take you wherever you want to go," Jon shouts above the noise.

Just then, I spy a sign with my name on it at the end of the Plexiglas wall.

"There. There it is!" I shout with excitement, but then my heart sinks knowing I will be parting company with Jon. I want to go with him, but good sense is screaming in my head at this point, insisting to be heard.

You just met him. You don't know him, and he didn't even remember your name. At least if this driver murders you, the hotel will know who to did it.

"Be sure he's the right guy!" Jon shouts. I confirm the driver's name and the hotel that sent him, trying not to show my disappointment that he was actually doing his job. Immediately, Carlos grabs my luggage and starts pushing me across the street dodging older models of compact cars.

But my eyes are on Jon. What is it about this man that has me mooning over my separation from him? No doubt he awakened something within me I had long thought was dead. An unexplainable electrical current passed between us, and I'm not ready to unplug myself. Besides, I didn't get a chance to say goodbye. I looked back through the traffic at the sight of him standing on the sidewalk looking for me.

"Thank you," I shouted to him, not really knowing what I was thanking him for.

"Call me!" he shouts.

"I will," I shout back as the sight of Jon vanishes behind a wall of traffic.

Something about him is fugazi, but I don't care. I want to see him again.

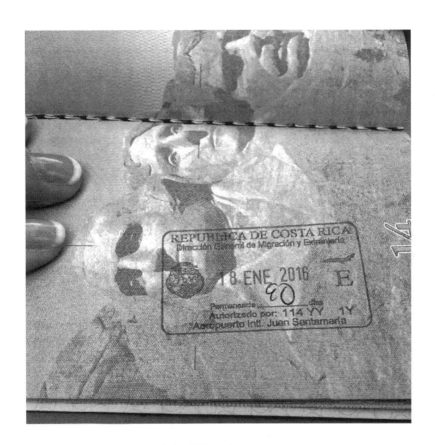

My First Stamp

HOTEL VILLA SAN IGNACIO

Carlos, my taxi driver, sent to fetch me from the hotel in Alajuela, is friendly and upbeat. His English is very good and his outgoing nature makes the journey to Hotel Villa San Ignacio quite pleasurable, albeit terrifying.

Car lanes and speed limits are mere suggestions here. Cars and buses spew exhaust and impatience as they speed along tight and narrow streets at breakneck speeds. Carlos is obviously no stranger to this practice. I plant my feet firmly against the floorboards and hold on to the handle above the door as he bobs and weaves through the streets to my hotel like he's Muhammad Ali behind the wheel of a car.

Carlos whips the steering wheel hard to the right and comes to a stop in front of an iron gate shouldered with terra cotta colored walls just a few feet off the busy main road.
"Villa San Ignacio," he announces proudly. The guard opens the gate and we enter an area that reminds me of my uncle's place in the heart of Miami, right off the main thoroughfare of US Hwy 1 yet you don't hear the traffic. A tropical paradise that feels like home.

The road inside the gate of Villa San Ignacio splits. To the left, it curves up the hill to a small building at the top. The road to the right runs above the hotel and you look down on its roof. Down a flight of stone-carved steps is the entrance to the hotel set under a green canopy of tall trees where a huge swimming pool is visible at one end. We take the road to the right.

Carlos hauls my bags down the steep embankment to the front desk.

"Hola! Como esta?" say two men in unison standing behind a desk.

"Muy bien, gracias," I reply, straightening my posture and

feeling accomplished in my superb command of the Spanish language.

Anthony, who checks me into the hotel, is a slender man with a warm easy smile and kind eyes. The hotel manager, Pablo, a shorter muscular blonde man with perfect English, accompanies him.

"Are you a transplant from the U.S.?" I ask Pablo.

He laughs. "Yes, what gave me away?"

"Your heavy accent," I said jokingly.

"I came here on a vacation. Went back to Colorado, sold everything, and moved here. I've never looked back. Let me show you around the hotel."

After introductions to members of the staff, Anthony hoists up only one of my bags. Nice guy but not terribly chivalrous.

"Come, I show you to your room." He leads me through the garden and up a flight of steps to my room on the second floor in a cluster of villas.

My room has an arched window and both it and the door are made of beautifully grained wood, stained a medium shade of brown. Inside is an ornate green iron queen size bed, understated nightstands, a bistro table set, and a tall wooden wardrobe straight out of C.S. Lewis' *The Lion, the Witch, and the Wardrobe.*

As senseless as it is, I can't fight the impulse to open up the large wardrobe door and feel the back of the cabinet. I don't know how I would have reacted if the back of the wardrobe had given way and opened. If I owned the place, I would not be able to resist cutting a door in the back of the wardrobe and having a trompe-l'oeil painting of "Narnia" on the wall behind it. The bathroom is equipped with a hair dryer and the usual amenities, but no television to be seen anywhere. I soon discover it is an unnecessary luxury.

I never put clothes into dressers when I travel, so I set my bags on the luggage rack next to the wardrobe and hurry downstairs in search of something to eat and drink, realizing that I haven't eaten since dinner the night before. I have no idea what time the kitchen closes here. I leave my room and head out to hunt food.

I walk through the foyer noticing details that had slipped my attention earlier. The foyer is more of a living room with over-stuffed furniture and a library wall full of books. I pass the front desk, but no one is there. I continue to the bar on my right. Walls seem to liquefy in this place with wide-open spaces to the outside just begging you to come out and play. I cross through the bar and find a table and chair overlooking the pool and sit down. Adjacent to my resting spot is a wooded area in which a gravel path winds into the forest and disappears.

The pool is large and pristine. The remains of the sun glints off of its surface, and the water begs me to come in, but with the sun going down, there won't be time for a swim since I don't see outdoor lighting. The wooded area to my right is teaming with wildlife; some I can see and some I can only hear. Multiple species of birds sit on the branches of the trees serenading me. I am alone but not lonely. This country is sweeping me off my feet, and I'm going to let it have its way with me.

Staring at the pool, I think of Jon joining me in a swim, and my mind wanders.

I untie the pareo from around my waist and let it drop to the ground exposing my skin to the warmth of the setting sun. I slip silently into the water and swim toward Jon entering the deep end of the pool.

"Ahem." I open my eyes to see Anthony from the front desk holding a menu. "So, you're the waiter, too?" I joke, wiping

43

the drool from my daydream.

"It seems that way, until someone else gets here. May I get you a drink? It is happy hour."

"Sure. Bring me something local."

Anthony disappears. I'm just settling back into my daydream with Jon when Anthony returns a few minutes later. He carries a delicious pink and orange frozen concoction made with Cacique. I thought it was just a fruit drink made of local fruits until the tipsy feeling confirmed the alcohol content.

"*Cacique Guaro,*" he says, "is sugar cane liquor and is best-selling distilled spirit in Costa Rica. It is the "Costa Rica liqueur."

I'll drink to that.

The actual waiter, Thomas, arrives and we discuss menu items.

"Only French and Italian offerings?" I ask. "Where's the Costa Rica food?"

"Oh, you mean the Tico food," he says with pride. "Down here," he points to the very small print at the bottom of the menu like on the Willie Wonka legal agreement that reads, "Typical Costa Rica dishes available upon request."

"I'm requesting!"

Poor Thomas didn't get the inference and stood there dumbfounded.

"Ah, I mean, please bring me a Tico meal," correcting myself.

I knew before the trip that dinner usually consisted of rice and beans, but I was still in a quandary. What do people eat here who are diabetic? What if they don't like beans? You probably become an employee in a hotel that serves French and Italian food!

I sip my drink as Thomas disappears, when out of the woods there arose such a clatter. No, wait, that's Santa Claus.

44

Maybe it's a sloth. Perhaps it is the Cacique, but I have myself convinced that a sloth will be crawling out of the woods.

Rats? No, not rats, but humans, a couple of them.

"Hello," say the young couple, "there's a beautiful path that winds its way through the forest. You should check it out after your meal."

"Tempting!"

Not tempting. I'm not wandering around out there in the dark without a flashlight. My adventurous side does have its limits.

You said you'd call him. Call him.

I swat the thought out of my mind like a gnat threatening to fly up my nose. I look down at my wrinkled hands with liver spots, and become aware of my butt cheeks hanging over the side of the chair.

Who are you kidding? Even if you lost fifty pounds, you'd still be old. Let him go.

Thomas shows up with my dinner. Scrambled eggs, rice and beans with spices and red peppers, salad, and fried plantains. Along with the food, he sets a bottle on the table that reads, "Lizano."

"What is that?" I asked pointing to the bottle, fearing this might be some sort of paste made from whorled lizard parts.

"Is made here in San Jose" he said.

"What's it for?"

"Everything!"

Putting aside my fear, I sprinkle a bit of the Lizano on my salad, tasting it for approval then scatter it all over my food. It doesn't taste like any salad dressing or sauce I've ever had, but Thomas is right—it tastes great on everything. The lizard is dead. Long live the Geico gecho!

After dinner overlooking the pool and bird watching in

the garden, I am disappointed that I didn't see a colorful quetzal bird. As darkness descends, I retire to my room. Entering my chamber, I instinctively reach to turn on the television. Then remember there isn't one. Not being able to zone out in front of a TV makes you realize just how much time is wasted watching the thing.

I try communicating on Facebook and looking at emails, but there is no Internet. Having no Internet connection makes you realize just how much time is wasted staring at your phone.

I recline on the bed, settling in to read a library book I had downloaded into my phone prior to this excursion, *Eat Pray Love* by Elizabeth Gilbert. It seemed an appropriate read for this trip. Three pages in, I fall asleep around 7:00 PM, still wearing the same clothing from the flight.

I awaken the next morning, cell phone stuck to my cheek, to the sound of birds singing, roosters crowing, and the smell of coffee brewing. I peel the phone from my face and look at the time.

It is only 5:30 AM! Oh, my God, is this how the entire trip is going to go—falling asleep with the pigeons and waking up at the butt-crack of dawn with the roosters?

I leave the room and follow the smell of coffee to the dining room downstairs. Hey, I'm already dressed.

What a beautiful, tranquil morning as I settle down at a table in the dining room facing the pool. My breakfast of full-bodied coffee, scrambled eggs, rice and beans, and toast gives me a taste of contentment. A few bites into my meal and the first three pages again of my book *Eat, Pray, Love*, when Carlos, my driver, suddenly appears in front of me.

"What are you doing? You're going to miss your bus!" Carlos says, losing his *pura vida*. I forgot he'd graciously agreed to take me to the bus station this morning to catch the bus north to La Fortuna, but I had completely lost track of time.

"Oh, my God. I can't miss the bus!" I fly up from the table and run toward my room, screaming at no one there as I pass the front desk, "I need to check out!"

"You haven't checked out yet?" Carlos squeals, throwing his arms in the air.

"There's been no one at the desk to do so!" I yell as I scale the steps to my room on the second floor. I grab things and toss them into my bags, helter-skelter. Thank God I hadn't unpacked the night before. I collect everything I can see and drag the bags down the stairs, clickety-clackety.

Carlos and a female, appear out of nowhere, discuss something in Spanish, and we dive into the car and head up the steep hill to check out.

It's perhaps a good thing that I am moving at the speed of light. I'm struggling with my internal voices who both want to call Jon and simultaneously not call Jon, and this skirmish is making the decision moot.

The checkout goes faster than rabbits get pregnant, and off we go. Carlos is doing an incredible job of weaving through the traffic toward San Jose and to the bus that will carry me north into the rainforest. We are making up lost time until suddenly the traffic comes to a dead stop, not unlike the morning rush hour traffic to Miami on I-95. Carlos and I heave a collective sigh of frustration, but can only sit and wait for the cars on the highway to start moving.

We aren't speaking much during this part of the journey. I have the distinct feeling Carlos is less than thrilled with me right now, and I think it best to keep my mouth shut. The upside is that the traffic jam stops his car directly across from the *Lizano* sauce manufacturing plant.

Yay.

We arrive at the bus station with little time to spare. Carlos lugs my bags up the escalator to the third floor ticket window. He quickly negotiates the transaction in Spanish for me. It's a whopping $5 charge to make the trip. Definitely a bargain. Back down the escalator we fly, ticket in hand, and Carlos points me through the turnstile toward the buses where I find the one that says "La Fortuna." The bus driver, speaking no English and obviously not experiencing "*pura vida*" that day, put tags on both of my bags, shoves them under the bus with other luggage, and hands me my claim tickets.

That's when it hit me — the coffee from this morning.

I try asking the bus driver my most important phrase I have been rehearsing for months before the trip, "*Donde esta el bano?*" but he either didn't understand plain Spanish or could care less because he just stares at me. I say it again, this time louder and more frantic. The crowd behind me says in unison, "Second floor." I look back at the bus driver who is still scowling at me, point to my wrist where a watch should be and say, "*Que*" not knowing if this is the correct word and not caring.

By this time, he must have gotten my sense of urgency and put up five fingers. I turn and haul ass up the escalator screaming, "*Donde esta el bano?*" at every person who looks at me and they point to the back corner of the second floor. As I slide in through the bathroom door, a maid yells something at me that sounds pretty emphatic, but I can't take the time to bother translating at this moment. I pass another woman standing at the sink, who tells me in English I have to pay to use the toilet.

"FINE!" I shout back as I fling the door open to a stall, lock it behind me, and pull at my clothing to sit down, just in time.

There's no toilet paper.

The English-speaking woman has departed the bathroom, and since I never practiced how to ask for toilet paper in Spanish,

I am left to my own devices.

Decorum and gentility prohibit me from continuing with the demeaning details, so suffice it to say, that I made it back to the bus with no help from the bathroom attendant just as the driver is ready to pull out of the station.

I am on my way to La Fortuna.

"Ma'am? Ma'am?" I open my eyes to see the steward/flight attendant or whatever they're called these days, standing over me in the aisle while holding a basket of snacks.

"Would you like a snack?" he asked.

"Ummm…do you have any blue potato chips?" I answer shaking myself out of my memory.

The flight attendant hands me a bag of the blue chips. Jon fought with our bags of chips on the flight over. It was a miracle chips didn't go flying all over the plane's cabin like startled bluebirds.

This time, however, my bag of chips yields to my efforts and comes open unceremoniously. I guess it's a sign that my adventure is coming to an end and that I don't need a man to complete my life or to open my bag of chips, for that matter.

But what if you want one? A man, not a potato chip. A companion. A soul mate. Someone with whom I can share the *pura vida*. People keep telling me that once I stop looking, I will find him. But how do you stop looking for something that's as essential to you as life itself? Do you stop looking for food when you're hungry or water when you thirst?

I munch on my blue chips and mentally sift through my high school philosophy courses for answers. I settle upon Aristotle, the Greek philosopher and scientist who coined the four elements. Since he couldn't conceive that the stars could be made out of corruptible earthly elements, he suggested a fifth element: æther.

My memory could be a tad fuzzy, but isn't that the stuff that puts you to sleep? Probably, since I had to fight to stay awake in those classes.

Then there's Hippocrates, who believed you couldn't live without balance. He said that an excess or a deficiency of bodily fluids directly influences the temperament a person can have.

Hippocrates believed certain human moods, emotions and behaviors were caused by an excess or lack of body fluids that he called "humors" in order for a person to be mentally and physically healthy.

I wonder if this is how The Three Stooges got their start in comedy. Experts thought they were full of shit, but actually, they were just full of humor.

Something is definitely jumbled up in my brain.

Hummm… So does this mean that my emotionally unbalanced attraction to Jon is really an excess of phlegm?

At any rate, I agree with Hippocrates in that we need balance in our lives, but with all due respect to both Aristotle and Hippocrates, I think there's gotta be one more element to make life worth living. One component just as essential as the other elements.

Love.

Tico Delicacies

MONKEY BRAINS

I snatch up the window seat directly behind my sour bus driver and put my backpack on the seat next to me. At the first stop, a pretty woman with a toxic attitude gets on, puts her hand on her hip, and glares at me from behind her very large bug-eyed sunglasses. I don't think I can take her if she jumps me, so I move my belongings off the seat. She plops her unhappy ass down next to me and starts taking selfies. I wonder if she's related to the bus driver. I have to say, until now, they have been the only two grumpy pusses I've met so far in Costa Rica.

Click.

The bus makes so many stops within the city that I begin to worry that I'm on the wrong one. Besides being old and rickety, the bus has torn vinyl seats and smells of urine and beer. No air ride comfort here. I realize it's been a while since I've taken public transportation. I haven't missed it. I was under the impression this was an express bus to La Fortuna. I guess I shouldn't assume things, especially for five dollars.

Click. This one's a side profile shot.

There's no air-conditioning on the bus so, I open the window to cool off. I watch the seemingly endless string of concrete walls, buildings, graffiti, and dust. Is this what the rest of the country looks like? Where is the beautiful lush green and fresh air Jon celebrated on the plane? Was the green of the airport volcano all there was to see?

Click.

The view out my window takes me back to downtown Miami in September of 1974 and my inaugural public bus ride to apply for a job with the public school system. The bus was in the same basic condition as this one, but with additional body odor of homeless people. With only the address of the building in

53

hand, I asked the driver to let me out when we reached the destination. I rode on for what seemed like hours, dropping off and picking up people along the way until the bus became empty. He pulled the bus over in an area under a highway overpass with concrete, graffiti, and dirt.

"This is the end of the line, lady."

"But this can't be the address I gave you. There's nothing here!"

"All you have to do is walk four blocks that way," he pointed his meaty finger in front of him, "and the place is on your left."

With that, he pulled on the handle opening the bus door and a "don't let the door hit ya in the ass on your way out" look. I stepped out of the bus onto the hot asphalt and blazing sun. To say I was not dressed for this environment would be a severe understatement. Never having gone to apply for a job before in my life, I wore a red and white plaid seersucker sundress barely covering my ass and four-inch espadrille wedges. It was the early 70s, remember? The bus drove off as I headed out in the direction the driver had indicated.

About one block and four blisters into my walk, I came across some sort of street construction and a police car. The officer waves me over from across the street.

"Miss. What are you doing here?"

I show him the address. "The bus driver said the building was that way and made me get off the bus."

"You cannot be in this part of town dressed like that. It's not safe. Go to that bar behind me and tell Tina that Mike the Cop told you to wait for him. I'll be off duty here in the next ten minutes, and I'll drive you safely where you need to go."

Well, now isn't that Miami hospitality!

I didn't think anything of it. I did as he told me to do. I was raised in a small town in Ohio, and my father always told me that if I was in any trouble, to look for a policeman and ask him for help.

A young girl walks into a bar…

I entered the dark bar and had to wait for my eyes to adjust. I could smell the beer and cigarettes, along with the sweaty patrons.

"Come over here, honey," came a raspy voice, not certain if it was a male or a female.

I walked like a blind person with my arms outstretched searching for something to grasp hold of. *I hope to God it's not a sweaty patron.* I could finally see a blonde woman behind the bar.

"What can I do for ya," she said.

"Mike the Cop told me to wait in here for him."

"Well, you just have yourself a seat here. Can I get ya some water?"

"Yes, please," I said feeling extremely out of place.

My eyes gradually adjusted to the dimly lit room and I could just begin to make out the people sitting around tables and the bar. A rough looking crowd to say the least, and they were staring at me sitting on that bar stool, all legs. I tugged at my dress but you can't make fabric grow and spandex hadn't been invented yet.

After what seemed like an eternity, Mike the Cop came in through the door. He walked me to his police car and drove me a few blocks down the road to the building to drop me off.

"Do you have a way to get home? Where are you staying, let's start with that," he said.

"I'm living with my uncle and aunt. I've got their address. I was gonna take a bus."

"Yeah, we see how well that worked out earlier. Let me see where they live."

I handed him the same paper with my destination, and on the reverse side, my aunt had written her address.

"Jesus Christ! You came all the way from here? You know you'll never make it back just on one bus, right? You'll have to change buses at least once to get home."

"I guess I didn't think this through very well," I said now starting to worry.

"Can you call them and see if one of them can come get you?"

"Well, no. My uncle works at the airport at night so he'll be on his way to work already and my aunt told me she was gonna be at the school for open house tonight. She's a principal." Each time I opened my mouth, I was sounding dumber and dumber. All that was missing was the blonde hair.

"Did they at least give you a key to get in the house?"

"Oh, yes," I said eagerly, happy to have gotten something right.

"Okay. I'll come back here in two hours. You should be done by then, and I'll take you home. You shouldn't be traveling alone by bus around here."

I'm beginning to wonder if I should have heeded that advice before boarding this bus here in San Jose, when the rackety machinery makes a big curve along the road and there it is — that fresh air Jon kept talking about. I inhaled until my lungs felt as if they might burst with cleanliness.

Jon has this same aroma. Why aren't I sitting next to him in his car? He would be a much better traveling companion than "Bug-eyed Betty" here. Call him.

No.

The bus enters a cloud feeling like a portal into another world. On the other side, I see the most stunningly beautiful mountains I've ever seen. Patches of green carpet the mountainsides as far as the eye can see. Built right alongside the two-lane road are small clusters of little concrete houses faded to pastels by the sun and topped with corrugated aluminum rooftops. They cling to the hillsides as if they too are climbing higher to escape the dust of the city. Even the doghouses have little corrugated roofs.

The parade of cars and trucks ahead of us grinds to a complete stop. I close my eyes as we sit motionless, willing the vehicles to once again climb the mountain. Finally, the procession crawls forward. Around the next bend, there are cows grazing on the steep hillsides. It's so vertical; it's almost inconceivable how they keep from toppling over and rolling down the steep incline into the crevasse. I swear the legs on one side of their bodies must be shorter than the other side just to stand upright.

Eighteen-wheelers, belching out their sooty opinions of this trek, take us past a white horse alongside the road chewing a mouthful of hay, indifferent to our struggle.

Is this the country's trusty white steed come to sweep me off my feet? Jon would look quite studdly sitting shirtless astride that steed.

My ears pop as we slog down one mountain, then up another, climbing ever higher.

Like the ruffles on a flamenco dancer's dress, we curl and swirl along the road as it dances through the mountains. There are roadside markets and little restaurants called "sodas," Mom and Pop businesses, selling food and drink. As the road twists to and fro, I can see both where we are headed and where we have been. I wonder if our path in life resembles this road from God's perspective, curling hither and thither trying to scramble our way to some elevated finish line we think we must attain. We need to look back to know where we have been in order to plot our course for the future, but I always feel like I take two steps forward then

57

three steps back, constantly wavering in my progress like the back and forth path of this road.

We stop again. Unlike the other drivers, the eighteen-wheeler in the lead seems unfamiliar with the swirls of this dance and everyone else begins blowing their horns in orchestrated accompaniment. I can't say that I blame the lead truck driver's trepidation; a two-lane road with severe cliffs on his left and the straight-up side of a mountain on his right. I'm so glad I chose not to rent a car and drive. That could have been me up there getting honked at in the front of the pack.

Looking out my window, we pass by a rectangular cloud hanging delicately over a deep ravine like a flag showing us how high we've climbed. It feels close enough to grab in my hand. A cotton ball on steroids.

Then, as if choreographed by Bob Fosse, everyone on the bus suddenly makes the sign of the cross upon their chests. Even Bug-eyed Betty stops her selfies long enough to form the sign across her very ample bosom, which seems to be the main attraction in her selfies.

As the bus moves into the bend to the left following the road, I can see out the windows up front and what is on the right side of the road. Tucked into the curve is a large concrete grotto enclosed by bars. Inside is an eight-foot tall crucifix complete with a full-color hanging, bleeding Jesus. Given that the ground drops off to a drastic cliff next to the bus, I question if they are crossing themselves out of reverence or fear?

The bus doesn't stop at the shrine to deposit any pilgrims, but continues swaying along the road in our trek north to the rainforest.

In a while, we come to what must be a bus stop since my dictionary doesn't recognize the words on the sign, and almost everyone leaves the bus except for me and a woman sitting across the aisle. I dip my toe into the conversation pool to test the waters and ask, "Habla ingles?"

"Si," she said laughing.

Oh, good, she speaks English.

"I'm going to La Fortuna. Can you tell me if this is the stop?"

"No, it will be the next stop."

"Oh, gracias!"

"Did you come here from America?" she asks.

"Yes, this is my birthday gift to myself." I am about to ask her questions about her knowledge of La Fortuna, but she turns to the man sitting next to her and begins talking in Spanish. I look at my phone. No service. So much for calling Jon.

People start coming back onto the bus, and I notice them handing the driver one of the cards he had given me at the onset of the journey. I guess it's like a hall pass or a "Get out of jail free" card. If I had known what it was for, I would have gotten off the bus to explore, but given the driver's attitude, he may have left me here.

An older woman with a warm and friendly smile steps onto the bus and replaces Bug-eyed Betty next to me. Although in reality, this short, round woman is probably my age. I check her roots.

I smile broadly and say, "Hola!" And with that, the race is on!

She speaks not a word of English and apparently doesn't understand my, "No entiendo," because she just keeps talking while I frantically look up words as quickly as she says them. The words come so fast that they blend together into what sounds like gibberish to my ears. People here talk like they drive, at a thousand miles a minute.

Her name is Rosa. She is a wearing a button-down white

shirt, a skirt and sensible pumps. She has wind-blown shoulder-length hair in a light rust color that appears to either be a recent dye job or her natural color — no gray. She reminds me of my first grade teacher, Mrs. Schmeltzer; huggable, cool green eyes, but with a gaze that lets you know she's a woman in control.

She unseals her bakery bag and offers me a white block of some kind of food. It looks like a cross between bread pudding and flan, but dryer.

I take a chunk. It could be monkey brains for all I know, but in some cultures it's considered an insult if you don't accept food offered to you, so I pop it into my mouth. Whatever it is, it's delicious. She offers her drink to me too, but I show her my bottle of water and she smiles and nods her head in understanding.

We travel along, she talks, I look up words, and both of us use our hands to gesture ideas. Playing a kind of Charades, Rosa moves her hands through the motions of her job, and I learn that she has been an anesthesiologist in a hospital for twenty years.

So, I take a crack at it, but I'm not nearly as good at this game as Rosa. I can't think of a universal sign for "Welcome to our office." I try using my dictionary, along with hand signals, but I'm not sure my gestures and words are clear. Either I just told her I work in an office for financial advisors or I told her I am here to rob a bank.

Rosa tells me to watch my luggage very closely when we get to La Fortuna. She points to the stunning landscape as she continues talking and I muster up a one-word sentence with "Beautiful." Rosa points to her ring finger on her left hand wanting to know if I'm married. How do you gesture, "Men consider me a pariah?" Rosa whips out her phone to show me photos.

Déjà vu. Jon showed me his family photos on the plane. It'd be my luck that she's Jon's mother.

I look at the pictures of her family, husband, children, and grandchildren. I take a second look at her children just to be sure I don't see Jon's face.

As we pull into the bus stop in La Fortuna, my very sweet, kind bus companion steps out into the aisle like a raging bull and blocks everyone from exiting the bus giving me time to get off first in order to capture my luggage. I leap out of my seat and spring for the door while yelling back over my shoulder to her, "Gracias! Gracias!"

Someone who appears to work for the bus system has the keys to the luggage compartment under the bus, and I am in his face yelling the only word I can remember for bag, "Bolso! Bolso!"

I frantically point to my two bags, holding up two fingers and shouting, "Dos! Dos!" This frenzied scene is only further exacerbated by a throng of young boys asking if they can carry my luggage and older men barking, "Who needs a hotel?" Still others are selling tours, water, snacks, and just about anything else nobody wants.

Each time I reach for my bags, the employee shoves my hand away and says something I don't understand. The throng of people standing around watching this scene finally join in a chorus of English yelling, "You have to give him the tickets first!"

Oh.

"lo siento," I offer up with a sheepish smirk.

With luggage in hand and my tail between my legs, I ask the store sales clerk my well-rehearsed sentence: "Donde esta le parade de taxi," assuming I will have to walk a mile to find a taxi stand. I am shocked and further embarrassed when the sales clerk points directly across the tiny street with a less than enthusiastic look that says, "Welcome, stupid tourist, to La Fortuna."

61

There is only one taxi and a couple is already at its window.

Crap! Now I'm gonna have to wait forever for another taxi. Why didn't I call Jon?

I kick myself for not calling him, but before I can get a really good self-deprecating harangue going, the couple walks away and the driver motions for me to come over. I will never know why the other couple walked away from the taxi. I like to think it is yet another sign that God is watching over me as another river is forged, but an even better one is yet to come.

HOTEL CAMPO VERDE

My heart sinks as my little red taxi skids through the gravel up a hill to the office of *Hotel Campo Verde*. It's little more than a tan wooden trailer, no bigger than a shed.

I pay the driver and he speeds off down the road. With baggage in hand, I climb the short stack of steps to the shed door and enter.

"Hola," I greet the young woman behind the desk.

I hope my cabin isn't as understated as this office.

"Hello."

English again. *They're making this too easy.*

"...and welcome to *Campo Verde*. My name is Oneida," says the beautiful caramel-skinned woman who checks me into the hotel.

"Here is a map of the grounds," she says. "You will be in Cabin number eight, which is here." She crosses an "X" atop my cabin on the map. "Walk down the driveway until you get to the sidewalk and follow it this way to your cabin." She draws a red ink line along the map.

"Would you be interested in taking a night hike up the volcano tonight?" Oneida inquired.

"Well, I already plan to do a night hike when I get to Monteverde."

"This one will be much better," she says. "You will see many things you won't see in Monteverde. Each part of the rainforest has its own things to see."

"Is there time for me to go to my cabin first?" I ask.

"Oh, yes, and you should get something to eat before you go, too."

I drag my bags behind me as I follow the gray gravel road onto a concrete path that runs along the top of a hill. Off to my right and down an embankment, is a green field with a herd of brown and white cattle, leisurely chewing grass and looking at me with casual indifference.

I wonder if I'm looking at next week's dinner entree.

I continue along the path to cabin number eight. A rolling overgrown field with cabins scattered all around comes into view, each facing a different direction. The vibrant green of the field and forest foliage, the fruit trees and the flowers leave me thinking I might as well be walking into the "shire" from the *Lord of the Rings*. I half expect to see a round Hobbit door at the entrance to my cabin. I look up.

"Oh, man, a volcano! I gotta learn to stop staring at the ground!"

One of my favorite TV characters, Gil Grissom on *CSI: Crime Scene Investigation*, could have been talking about me when he said, "People never look up." For the first time since I exited the hotel office, I lift my head and gasp at the sight of Volcán Arenal looming above me. I'm so used to looking down at my phone or just at eye level like I do in South Florida that I'd forgotten the world isn't flat! Obviously, I knew the volcano was in the vicinity, but never dreamed I'd be sitting cross-legged at its feet.

Like a devotee of a charismatic cult leader, my heart begins to beat faster and I feel my face flush with excitement at being so close to this powerful and dangerous force.

My fascination with volcanoes started in elementary school while looking through history books. I became mesmerized by the destruction of Pompeii. The people became entombed in ash, rock, and lava as they went about their normal daily activities when Vesuvius suddenly and ferociously erupted. This fixation also led to an obsession with the minds of serial killers, but that's a story for another time.

64

Like every other kid in grammar school, I had to come up with a science project. For my fifth grade venture, I built an erupting volcano diorama. It became a family affair with my father's structural design suggestions, my mother's help in the kitchen mixing up the salt dough, and my artist brother drew out a landscape for me to duplicate. It looked fantastic, but was super heavy, and I would need help carrying it to school.

"What are you gonna use to make it erupt?" my father asked.

"Baking soda and vinegar," I replied confidently like I had just discovered a new chemical element.

My father curled his upper lip in lack-luster approval. "I got something that'll be more like the real thing. I'll bring it home tomorrow."

"But, I have to take this to the teacher tomorrow," worried I would miss the deadline for turning in my project.

"Don't worry about it. You can't carry it anyway. I'll carry it to the school for you since it's so heavy. When's your turn to show the teacher how it works?"

"Tomorrow, and I'm first!"

With that, my father went off to work the 3-to-11 shift in the lab at the paper mill.

The next morning, Dad carried my volcano to the classroom along with a clear glass baby food jar filled with what looked like orange Tang.

"What's that?" I asked.

"It's your lava," Dad answered with a smirk.

I knew that smirk. It meant I was either getting an "A" or I was gonna crash and burn in the lava along with the green plastic army men glued to the landscape at the foot of the volcano. I crossed my fingers as we went off to school.

"And now, class," said the teacher, "Teresa is going to

show us her volcano project, and she's brought her father to help her."

"Here," my father said slipping me the glass baby food jar. "When we get up there, you pour a little of this into the top of the volcano. Just a little."

In Dad's design, he had me use an empty tuna can for the center of the volcano so it wasn't too deep of a hole. Around that I had wadded up newspaper as support for the sides of the volcano then draped the salt dough over that.

Once at the front of the classroom, Dad sat the project on a low table, and he gave me the nod to add the contents of the jar — just a little.

Unfortunately, shaky little hands and contents that wouldn't pour gently resulted in the majority of the contents of the jar plopping out into the tuna can in a heap. I looked up at Dad in fear that I had ruined things, and he shook his head from side-to-side and crinkled his nose, wordlessly saying, "Not to worry." Then he smirked.

"I am going to show what happens when melted rock or magma from the upper mantle layer, here, deep inside the earth pushes up through a crack in the earth's crust and explodes out through the volcano," I recited my research while pointing to my board drawings.

After finishing my talk, I looked up at Dad not knowing what was supposed to happen next, figuring he had a bottle of vinegar in his pocket to squirt onto the orange crystals.

Instead of a bottle, he pulls out a kitchen match, strikes it against something rough in his hand, and touches it to the orange crystals.

The flame from the match made the crystals ignite and spew sputtering, crackling sparks and flames up into the air about two to three feet. Then the burned and blackened ash from the crystals fell back down onto the volcano and its surrounding landscape, burying the army men and trees in black soot.

As the volcano erupted, so did the classroom, not to mention the teacher. I backed up with silver-dollar size eyes staring at the display of blackened carnage, and looked up at my father whose belly was jiggling from laughter with his tongue pressed through the empty space in his mouth covering up his missing tooth, overcome with knee-slapping joy.

I received a "B" on the project for accuracy in my demonstration but, with the proviso that my father promise to never assist me on science projects again.

Standing on the front porch of Cabin number eight, I drop my things and stare up at the Beast. At a mile high, clouds obscure the top of Volcán Arenal, a frequent occurrence for this model-perfect specimen. But this isn't just any 'ole volcano. This one's a serial killer.

For five hundred years the surrounding villagers thought Arenal was just a photogenic mountain. I'm trying to wrap my head around the shock and terror they must have experienced in the early morning hours in 1968 as volcanic rocks and ash rained down from the skies killing eighty-eight people. A few small villages – Tabacón, Pueblo Nuevo, and San Luís—were either partially or completely destroyed. I flash back to photos of Pompeii and its unfortunate townspeople. Would I have survived if I had been one of the inhabitants here or in Pompeii? No doubt I would've had a serious case of nerves, provided I lived through the experience.

Looking at it now, serene and green, it's hard to imagine that kind of devastation from this volcano considered a youngster at just over 7,000 years old. Following the explosion in

1968, it stayed active for forty-two years as it continued to belch up volcanic eruptions several times a day with remarkable nocturnal emissions of red-hot lava flows that you can see in videos online.

Sounds like an indigestion problem. I need a Tums.

Tourists flooded the area and many of them, as well as guides, and at least two planes full of passengers perished on the sides of Arenal trying to get a closer look. Stupid choices to get so close, but I understand the strange attraction. Somehow the immense power and potential for danger draws us in like the proverbial moth to the flame in spite of our good sense. Is it the "living life on the edge" adrenalin burst that pulls us in or the "stop and stare fatal attraction" that makes us face our own mortality?

Considering these deaths, you would think people would move away and stop living beneath this killer, but instead they set aside farming in lieu of tourism as a more lucrative source of income as throngs of people flooded La Fortuna to observe the spectacle.

Not to disappoint, in 2010, a large avalanche occurred along the southwest flank of Arenal, followed by a significant lava flow. That seems to have been its last violent outburst since seismologists think that Arenal has gone into a resting phase that should last approximately 800 years—"should" being the operative word. That just means it's not currently erupting.

I hope seismologists are more accurate than the meteorologists on the evening news.

I think about how Volcán Arenal is part of the Pacific Ring of Fire, a mind-boggling area of deadly volcanoes shaped like a huge horseshoe in the Pacific Ocean and cringe at the combined destructive power within that basin. Arenal Volcano has been ranked among the top ten historically active volcanos in the

68

world, and I'm on the north side of it.

Jonny Cash's "Ring of Fire" plays through my mind as I turn my attention to my home for the next couple of nights—unless I perish in molten lava.

My bungalow has a covered porch with two rocking chairs and a small table directly facing the volcano. I open the front door to a huge vaulted, brown wood-beamed ceiling with two queen-size beds, AC, a shower big enough for three people at a time, and a sit-in bay window framing the volcano smack-dab in the center of the glass. It's just like the bay window seat in a book from my youth that I must have read fifteen times called *The Velvet Room* by Zilpha Keatley Snyder.

The sheltering of thick velvet in the room of an abandoned house during the Depression becomes a source of solitude and a much-needed escape into an enchanted world for a poor young girl. Although this window seat isn't covered in velvet like the one in Snyder's book, its presence in this room provides a sense of comfort, and the view of the volcano seduces me towards that window bench. I can't wait to settle in there with a cup of coffee...

...and contemplate my potential demise in a volcanic pyroclastic flow of Biblical proportions like my green plastic army men, who never saw it coming.

Call him. You promised him you would.

Hearing no internal dissention not to call, I close my eyes and allow my mind to drift away as I picture Jon's soft green eyes looking deeply into mine, remembering the touch of his hand as he takes me into his robust arms and...

"Would you like something to drink, Miss?"

The voice jolts me out of my daydream like a fork in a toaster.

"Uh....uh....uh," I stammer trying to remember where I

am. I find myself sitting at an outdoor table of a restaurant across the street from my hotel.

How did I get here?

It is the only place within walking distance to get food. Oneida, in the hotel office, arranged for me to go on a night hike tonight through the jungle at *Ecoglide Arenal Park*, and I needed to eat. I had crossed the two-lane highway fearing for my life from the Daytona-speeding drivers and am now on the veranda of the restaurant.

"I'm so sorry! I was lost in thought and didn't hear you walk up. Uh, I only see menu offerings of American food. Do you offer Tico dishes?"

"Yes, ma' me. And to drink?"

"Iced tea, no lemon, please."

Call him now!

I look up the number Jon gave me and press call.

Oh, my, God! Oh, my, God! Oh, my, God! Oh, my, God! Oh, my, God! Oh, my, God!

"Hello?"

HE ANSWERED.

Hang up, you idiot, hang up! What are you going to say? All the teen-like raging hormones awaken and are in full bloom.

"Jon, it's Teresa, from the plane," I said in the most seductive tone I could muster, my voice catching in my throat and coming out two octaves higher than it should.

"Oh! Hello! Where are you?" he asked.

He remembers me! He wants to know where I am! He's going to drive up here and we'll dance hand-in-hand, merrily along the banks of the Balsa River.....errrrr! SLAP! My adversarial voice just coldcocked the ditzy romantic living in my head.

"I'm in La Fortuna at the hotel…"

He suddenly interrupted me and said, "Can I call you back

in a few minutes?"

"Um, sure, of course," I said, and the call went dead just as a huge vulture swooped down out of the trees and glided right past me.

That can't be a good sign.

"Your iced tea, miss," says the waiter as he placed a tall dessert glass in front of me containing a tan frozen drink with a straw in it. I just sit there staring at it for several seconds wondering if I should try finding the Spanish words for "iced tea" since this obviously didn't look anything like iced tea. I ventured a taste, and sure enough, it was iced tea, but in the form of a frozen smoothie.

I keep forgetting I'm not in Kansas anymore, Toto.

Ice Tea

ECOGLIDE ARENAL PARK

I pass the mirror in my cabin and pause. *Am I really doing this?*

It's just before dusk, as I prepare to climb into a van from the *Ecoglide* tour company. I'm alone in a foreign country preparing to venture up a volcano and explore the rainforest in the dark. Same face and hiking boots as when I left Florida, but the person inside is barely recognizable.

Who are you? I ask of myself and head for the door.

"Hola. Como esta?" I greet the driver as I bend over trying not to hit my head on the van door. There's no one else inside the new and spotless vehicle.

I must be first. It's always fun to be in first place.

The van makes no more stops, though, and eventually pulls into a dirt clearing next to a building bearing the name *Ecoglide Arenal Park*. Where are the other tourists?

"Excuse me," I lean forward, "where is everyone else?"

"No one else signed up. You're it," said the driver as he pulled away leaving me in the darkening, dusty field.

Heading toward the building, I entered the glass doors and walked up to the cashier who says, "You will be treated to a private tour of the jungle."

"Oh, that's outstanding! Can you tell me if the Maleku Village is far from here? I'm looking to purchase some of their artwork," I ask.

"Not far, but closed now."

One of the things on my "To Do" list while in La Fortuna is to visit the Maleku Village, a working village showing how the people in Costa Rica survived for many years. The Maleku are artisans and farmers and create Balsa woodcarvings, "masks," which represent the creatures in Costa Rica and the meaning they hold in their community. Onieda, from the hotel front desk, is diligently working to get me into the Maleku village to meet some of the people, find out about their lives, and buy some of their artwork to take home.

A swarthy young man with thick black hair, about my height with a toned body, and smiling eyes approaches me.

"Buenas noches. I am Robert. I will be your guide for tonight's hike. I heard you asking Rosa just now about the Maleku Village. I am a member of the Maleku."

"Yes, oh my God, I know of your people."

Good God, did I just say that? Who am I, Moses?

"I read about you, well, them before I came. This is so awesome!"

Robert's face lit up. He must have been happy to hear that I already knew of the Maleku.

"Are you ready to head out? Here is a flashlight for you. Do you need water or insect repellant?"

"No, I'm all set."

We step out into the dark with our flashlights sending out beacons of hope like little lighthouses promising my safe return. The temperature was not too hot and the humidity was low. That'll change once we start hiking.

"Where are you from," asked Robert.

"Florida. This is my first trip outside of the United States."

"Why are you alone?"

"I wanted to come by myself. That way you can go where you want and not have to deal with someone else's issues."

"You have no husband? No boyfriend?"

"Nope. Divorced many years ago," I explained. "And what about you? Do you have a family?"

"No, and I don't want one! I'm only thirty-one, and I'm getting pressured to marry some woman of another tribe and

74

start a family," he said. "I don't even date! There are only 650 Maleku remaining in the country, and I guess I'm supposed to repopulate the place! I must marry outside of my community because all the Maleku are now related. I don't want to get married right now!"

"Maybe your parents...are they still alive?"

"Yes."

"Well, maybe they just want some grandchildren."

We laughed realizing his culture is not unlike an Italian family pushing for grandchildren, and that the peoples of the world may not be so different after all.

We continue the steep incline up the volcano. I'm already winded.

Good God, do I have what it takes to do this?

Our first encounter in nature as we walk the trail is with an industrious band of leaf cutter ants carrying their harvest of leaves like a group of racing board surfers on Biscayne Bay. They scurry in well regimented lines, some passing the slower participants, their "sails" hoisted high above their bodies, swaying gently from side-to-side.

We stop and bend down to watch more closely. Robert explains, "The worker ants cut the leaves stimulating new plant growth, and will carry some up to three times their body weight into their underground shelters to cultivate their own fungal garden, sometimes up to two meters deep, from which they feed. Neither the ants nor the fungus can survive without each other. The ants are only part of a three-way," Robert says raising his eyebrows in a suggestive joke, "symbiotic relationship."

Is this kid coming on to me?

The beam of light from our flashlights attracts numerous flying things, and I wave them from my face with my left hand.

Mosquitoes the size of door keys. Check and swat.

"The fungus garden can only grow through the ants' farming skills. However, the ants' fungal garden is susceptible to a parasitic fungus that can form a white growth rendering the ants' garden inedible, and so the colony dies. BUT—and here's the really cool third part of the three-way—the female ants' bodies grow a particular type of bacteria that they spread over their garden and it kills the parasitic fungus. This particular bacteria is also found in more than half of the world's antibiotics used today. From farmer to fungi to pharmacist!"

Leaf cutter Ants. Check.

The terrain is getting steeper. I sip from my CamelBak hydration backpack and surge on. Robert shows me a yellow-breasted, brown winged bird with a black mask who isn't the least bit afraid of us as it sits on a branch just inches from my face. I reach for my notepad to write down its name, but before I can find it, Robert starts talking again.

"Do you see it?" Robert asks.

"See what? The bird?"

"No. The jumping viper, the snake right there." He points to a pile of leaves at the base of a tree only two feet beside me.

I freeze. I don't dare to breathe except in short, shallow gulps of air, forgetting to exhale. Fear from decades ago floods my mind with the terrifying memory.

Robert pulled me away from the pile of leaves, a short distance from the tree.

"Are you all right?" he asked. He was truly surprised at my response.

Still quivering with adrenaline, I struggle to answer, my mouth dry, "SNAKE! It was gonna bite me."

"No, I wouldn't let that happen."

"You don't understand," I said, clasping his upper arms. "I...I was about four years old playing in the garage of our home
76

in the country. The garage door was shut to keep out the heat, and I was prancing around pretending to be a unicorn or something, when I had that feeling of being watched. I stopped and stood very still, listening to see if my mother had called me. I looked to the stairs leading up to the kitchen, but she wasn't there.

"I scanned the room from the stairs, past the back door, and over to the workbench. My eyes rose slowly toward the ceiling. That's when I met another's gaze.

There, dangling about a foot above my head was a huge rattlesnake, wrapped numerous times around the garage door track. Its brown and black scaly body was as big around as my young child's thigh. With feet frozen to the floor, I was barely breathing, too scared to make a sound or flinch a muscle."

Robert's face grew serious, his eyes wide with concern. "What happened?"

"Mom called down the stairs to me, but I couldn't answer. She walked down a few steps to where she could see me, and said, 'Why aren't you answering me? Look at me when I'm talking to you...' she followed my gaze, and I heard her gasp as she saw the snake. She whispered, 'Don't move.'

"Mom went back up the stairs, screamed at my uncle to get his gun. Uncle Bob slowly descended the steps, gun in hand, but he couldn't take the shot 'cos his hand shook so badly. He told my mom the bullet might ricochet off the track or the ceiling and hit me.

"Afraid to blink, locked into the hypnotic trance of the snake's yellow cat-like eyes, I remained paralyzed. Seeing my uncle couldn't help, Mom called for backup.

"Backup? Who was going to get there in time?" Robert asked, making me take a drink of water. I drew a long gulp from my hydration tube.

"She called David, the neighbor down the road who got there in seconds. Stepping silently down the stairs, he carried his bow and arrow.

"David took aim and released the arrow as my uncle grabbed me, pulling me toward the stairs. David's marksmanship was deadly accurate. The arrow plunged into the snake's neck and it fell writhing to the garage floor."

"I know why you were scared back there," said Robert, his eyes now warm and calming.

I don't know for sure if that snake was truly laying there perfectly camouflaged under that tree, or if Robert was playing a cruel joke on me, but as an old boyfriend used to say: "Be it arson or accident, the results are the same." No tip for you.

Jumping viper. Didn't see it, don't care if I do. Check.

Once my breathing returns to normal and with some reassurance that the danger is passed, we set off again to hike the trail up the base of the volcano. The forest is dry, not moist like I expected, and aside from mosquitoes buzzing past my ear, it's quiet. Not what I anticipated at all. The trees are so tall and the leaf coverage so thick that it feels like there's a ceiling over my head, like walking through a cave. Robert shines his flashlight through the blackness into distant trees and points out two hidden, sleeping toucans. Their eyes part slightly, looking at us with disdain for interrupting their slumber. Even far away, they are huge. The beams of light illuminate their shiny black feathers and the dark chestnut color on their large beaks.

"Those are Black Mandibled, also called Chestnut Mandibled Toucans," Robert said. "They are the largest of the six species of toucans in Costa Rica."

"I would never have seen those toucans if it hadn't been for you, Robert," I struggle to say as I gasp for air. "Is *everything* here in the rainforest camouflaged?"

Robert laughs as he grabs my elbow and pulls me along. "Pretty much. Blending into the surroundings is protection from being someone's dinner."

Toucans. Check.

Hiking farther along the trail, Robert jumps down onto a ledge next to a stream, rustles a few leaves, and moves a large piece of tree bark lying on the ground. He springs forward and comes up with a tiny frog in his hands. Robert hops effortlessly back up to where I am standing on the trail. This Maleku man is part frog himself.

The striking brilliant yellow and royal blue of the frog glistens in the light of my flashlight as he hops up onto the lapel of Robert's jacket, posing nicely for pictures as if the two of them have this choreographed dance every night.

"You can't touch this. I can because I'm used to it," Robert cautioned me, "I've become immune to its toxin."

He just earned back his tip.

Poison Dart Frog. Check.

Robert drops back down to the piece of tree bark and gingerly places the poisonous frog back where he found him. We continue up the trail.

The incline increases, and I stop frequently to catch my breath. Robert waits patiently as he collects numerous plants to show me how his people use them in daily life.

He tears off a tiny, five millimeter piece of a leaf and says, "Here, chew this."

I pop the leaf into my mouth without a second thought as to the potential dangers it might hold. Immediately, my entire mouth, throat, and tongue go numb.

"The Maleku use this plant as an analgesic," he explains, "maybe for anyone needing oral surgery."

Now I begin to think I could be in trouble. I try to

79

remember what pocket holds my whistle.

*Oh. My. God. You're alone in the woods with no idea of which way to run with a man who could kill you by hurling a poison dart frog at your face and now you can't even scream for help. What the hell are you doing out here? Are you insane? Duh, duh-gha-ghaa...*My adventurous self just crammed one of these leaves down the throat of my voice of reason.

Robert casually continues to show me other plants, the ones used as soap for cleaning clothes, some for curing ailments, and others used for food while I try to regain my ability to speak.

I wonder if this plant has affected my airway. Is it closed? Can I breathe? Of course you can breathe, you dipstick, otherwise you'd be face down on the dirt.

His body language doesn't indicate anything threatening, so I stop considering where I put my whistle and start listening to Robert talk again. Eventually, my mouth regains feeling and my voice comes back.

"My God, that plant was impressive! How did you know I wouldn't be allergic to it?"

"I didn't," he smirks and turns back towards the trail. There goes that tip again.

"One animal I so want to see is a sloth, but it doesn't seem to be happening tonight," I whine to Robert. Although he keeps his keen eyes peeled for one, there aren't any in the area.

Must be bowling night for the sloths.

We make our way back to the dusty clearing where the van is waiting to take me back to my hotel. Hours had passed in the forest that seemed like minutes. Time flies when things are trying to kill you.

"Robert, thank you so much for your excellent tour," I say slipping a twenty into his hand as I board the van back to my hotel still longing for the Maleku masks I am anxious to purchase, but they're proving to be as elusive as the sloths.

Back in my hotel room, the sweat and bug repellant propels me towards the shower. The water feels incredibly refreshing against my skin after the strenuous hike through the forest. Alone in the waterfall of the shower I let my mind wander to thoughts of Jon.

"May I join you?" I hear him say.

"Of course. I'll never turn down help washing my back." He takes the washcloth from my hands and begins making soapy circles across my shoulders. The suds slide down my back and over my hips, dropping in soft plops onto the shower floor.

"Is this the way you like it?"

"A little lower, if you don't mind."

BIRDS OF A FEATHER

Sunrise comes earlier in Costa Rica than in South Florida. I should be sleeping in, but I can't get enough of this country and don't want to miss a minute of it. I throw on shoes and head out for breakfast.

I stop along the gravel road just before reaching the dining room next to a tree teeming with brightly colored birds. The old adage is, "Birds of a feather, flock together," but Spanish birds must hold to a different saying. I'm shocked that so many bird species are gathered together and not fighting over the seed in the feeder. A lesson for South Floridians waiting in lines for ice following a hurricane.

As I admire the smorgasbord of fowl, a woman walks over to where I am standing.

"Oh, my, the colors are stunning, eh?" she says.

French Canadian judging by the accent. They must have missed the turnoff for South Florida and just keep flying southward.

"I agree," I say. "I'm exceptionally taken by that black one," pointing at one in particular, "that one with the brilliant red on his back, but I don't know what he is." I dig through my backpack for my bird field guide.

"Yes, I'd say he's the most dynamic of the group," she says.

"Oh, look, I think I found him." I hold up a page of the guide and point to a photo.

"What it says there, 'Cherries Tanager?'" She squints at the small print under the photograph.

"Yeah, I think you are right," I said nodding my head in agreement.

She points to a clay-colored bird, "How can that one be so

plain and that Cherries one be so brilliant?"

"Well, it's not uncommon in the bird world for the female to be less attractive than the male," I say sounding like I know what I am talking about.

"I know some couples like that," she jokes.

We stand there until our stomachs get the best of us, then head in for breakfast.

As I open the door to the dining room, the appealing aroma of freshly brewed coffee fills the air. The room is little more than an addition onto the side of the office shed, but clean and inviting with lace-covered tablecloths and sunny yellow napkins on the tables. A small vase of flowers and soft music bring a cheery brightness to the room. The Canadian woman sits down at a table with her friends as I make my way to an open table in the rear. Breakfast is hot and Tico—scrambled eggs, rice and beans, with a side of fresh fruit. The music faded into the background as I listened to the conversations taking place around me. Drifting from each table are the lyrical sounds of different languages blending together into an international buffet of speech—French, German, some form of Asian, Russian, Spanish, and something Scandinavian. I could see us all as if we are the birds out in that tree, all unique but each adding to the *joie de vivre* of humanity. I wonder if birds experience the same language differences at their breakfast "branch" or do they instinctively understand each other. Does, "Harriet, pass the salt" in say, Cherries Tanager, sound different when chirped in parakeet?

While I sip my coffee, I flash back to my second child around the age of nine. She presented a fifteen-minute illustrated talk for 4-H, "She's Wearing a Dead Bird on Her Head!" based on a book by the same title. Her talk focused on the declining numbers of birds in Florida due to extremes of fashion and the haughty pretensions of society in the 1880's. More than five million birds were being massacred yearly as frenzied fashionistas insisted on wearing aigrettes and other plumage on their hats. The fashion industry went so far as to stuff entire birds and turned them into haute headwear. I try picturing myself in the late 1800's selecting one of these birds for my milliner. Would I have been a party to this fashion trend? Could I have perpetrated such insensitivity against these helpless and beautiful creatures? I like to think not.

"Mommy, how could people kill birds to wear on their heads? Did they eat the birds?" my daughter asked. She was shocked to learn that not only did they not kill the birds for food, but that women were not permitted to vote in the 1800's, thereby drowning out the opportunity to voice their opposition to this practice. It was a close second as to which one disturbed her more.

This absurd headwear choice was not only an egregious act committed against birds, but hurt the women's suffrage movement. How could anyone take seriously a woman arguing for the right to vote while wearing a dead bird on her head? Fashion was "killing it" in more ways than one. Funny how an idea that seems to make sense in one time period becomes ludicrous in another — both in choice of headwear and the right to vote.

After eating, I head back to the tree buffet to see if I can identify more feathered diners. It seems impossible, but there appear to be even more birds on display. My heart aches at the thought of them atop a person's head. How are so many in one small tree? Are they *glued* onto the branches? I look for tethers to see if they have been tied there. Nope. How is this tree even standing under the weight of them all?

A German woman whom I had heard speaking with her

friends at breakfast joins me to observe the stunning display. She has a camera.

Damn it! I don't have my phone or my camera. I never dreamed I would see something while on my way to breakfast that would make the Audubon Society drool. Note to self: always carry camera.

"Oh, you're so smart to have your camera with you," I smiled at the German woman.

"Ich spreche kein englisch."

I never learned German from my paternal grandmother, but I guess she has no clue what I'm saying.

I whip out my bird guide again and start searching for the autumn orange and flame-colored bird with a white and black head and yellow breast. A "Great Kiskadee" according to my guide. I share the field guide photo and name with the woman, but she just smiles and says, "Danke" or something I am guessing that means, "get out of my face."

The clay-colored Thrush I had seen earlier was still gorging himself on the seed alongside the Cherries Tanager. But, they have now been joined by a green and yellow bird named the "Orange-chinned Parakeet" and a black-breasted bird with red wings and a white spot on his cheek called a "Montezuma Oropendola." The names are almost as exotic as their adornment.

I check the time and realize I'm going to be late for the van to my next escapade if I don't break away from my feathered friends and hurry on to my cabin. As I scurry down the road, I consider what I would be called should I have a bird name. "Hot Fudge Pudgy" might just suit the bill.

THE HOWLER MONKEY

"Pura Vida!" I shout as I don my bathing suit, feeling certain I will be getting soaking wet somewhere along the beautiful Balsa River while white water rafting. Although the river holds only a Class II ranking in difficulty, I am not about to let the amateur status diminish the excitement for this once-in-a-lifetime birthday gift to myself.

The moment is short lived, however, as I look in the mirror and see the beginnings of the underbrush in my nether regions. I feel annoyed at its reappearance so early into the trip, and feel my *pura vida* slipping away. My pre-trip pruning should have lasted me for the duration of this excursion, but there it is poking through my skin — hair like a howler monkey.

Over the years, I have tried trimming, waxing, shaving, and letting it grow, but hair *down there* continues to be a curse into my sixties. Coping with it in my younger years was an ordeal, but back then, I had the ability to fold myself in half to view the area in question for maintenance; except when I was pregnant, of course.

When you're first pregnant and still have the ability to see your feet, you can proficiently trim the lowland areas yourself, given a small but sharp pair of scissors or razor and a hand-held mirror. This, however, gives you a false sense of achievement because as the pregnancy progresses, one day, as you go to do some grooming, you realize you can no longer see the land down under. This is when you realize, you are not an island unto yourself and you need an intervention.

However, the thought of ripping out hair from my most delicate body parts while carrying a child inside of me sounded like something close to infanticide, and I dismissed the whole concept of waxing. This left me with the need to find another outside source that I could trust to trim the hedges. Wishing the task on ANY of my friends was repulsive and played too close to an article out of *Hustler* magazine for my tastes, which left me with my only other option — my then husband.

I am pleased to say, his barbershop mastery fit the bill through three pregnancies…almost. It was with my last pregnancy, when I was HUGE that things went south. Literally. Whether it was because my size eclipsed the sun's rays or because my now aging husband's eyesight was failing, it happened…he slipped and the tip of the scissors sliced into my delicate skin causing great obscenities to fly. It took a bit of pinching of the incision to make the bleeding stop, but stop it did. Note: don't try applying Band-Aids to that area unless you want to inflict additional pain and suffering.

The following week, at my routine gestational appointment, with feet in stirrups and physician beginning his inspection, I had forgotten about the near-fatal disfigurement my husband had inflicted upon my genital area.

My OB/GYN, Dr. Maheswaran, was a very steady, quiet speaking, and no-nonsense type of man. Without looking up at me, he gave the cut a gentle tap and said, "I see you cut yourself. I wouldn't recommend you trying to do this yourself," as apparently I was *not* the only female looking to solve this grooming dilemma. "Have your husband do it for you," he added.

"My husband's the one who cut me!" I exclaimed, quickly throwing him under the bus.

"Then tell him he's out of a job until he gets his eyesight checked," the doc said sternly, but with a sly grin to the side of his mouth.

Well, standing around staring at yourself in the mirror isn't working. How in the hell am I gonna fix this out here in the rainforest? Maybe the hotel has a spa.

I pick up the phone to the front desk.

"I need an intervention, err, no, I mean, do you have a salon in the hotel?"

"Salon? You mean for hair?" she asked.

"Definitely for hair! Uh, no, I mean, ummm, for waxing, you know," my voice trailing off into a whisper.

"Oh, the bathing suit area, you mean?"

"Yes," I expel a puff of relief.

"No, I am afraid not," she said.

I hung up the phone and go back to the mirror.

Now what? I bit my lip.

If I were Superman, I could use my laser vision and burn it off. I think it might just work if I reeeally concentrate.

I open my eyes wide and stare intently, willing laser beams to explode from my eye sockets. I think the only thing that explodes is a blood vessel. Amazing the shit you'll try when you're desperate.

Tweezers?

Oh, hell no! Keep thinking, dammit! I scold myself as I dig through my bags searching for a razor or a pair of scissors, even.

What hotel doesn't have a spa?

God, I'm even willing to be waxed again if you'll just let a salon drop out of the sky right now.

How could I have forgotten to bring a razor? I continue digging in my bags.

"Ah-ha," I say triumphantly holding up my very sharp camping knife.

Are you nuts? You can't even peel an apple without coming close to severing your thumb. I put the knife away, exasperated.

After upending everything in my Costa Rica hotel, I

realize the trimmer is back in the US.

I brought a knife but forgot a razor. *Nice going.*

The hotel has no spa, and the van to take me rafting will be here any minute, but I can't be seen like this.

Well, what's it going to be, girl? Are you going to miss out on an opportunity of your lifetime just because of a few, okay, several hairs?

In my younger years, the answer would have been to cancel the trip, and not risk ridicule by strangers. But, not today, not at this stage in my life.

Something is happening inside of me.

With renewed enthusiasm for the adventure, I fish out a pair of quick-drying shorts to cover up the rapidly emerging shrubbery, and with a shout of, *"Pura Vida!"* the Howler Monkey heads to the river.

WHITE WATER RAFTING

My rafting guide with the *Desafío* tour group, Elmer, is knowledgeable and outgoing. He helps me gear up with my helmet and life vest.

"Keep these straps tight," he said while pulling the vest straps tightly around my torso, "they will loosen up once they get wet."

We are a large crowd divided into individual groups of four or five. Elmer pulls into his rafting mates a husband and wife couple from Chicago and me. Like a flight attendant running us through procedures on a plane, Elmer quickly runs us through our instructions on how to paddle, and what he expects from us with each command. The mental image of his stocky, muscular body dressed as a flight attendant flashes through my mind, and I snort at the visual.

"When I say, 'Paddle right,' the people on the right side of the raft paddle hard," he instructed. "If I say, 'Get down,' that means you drop to the floor of the raft with your paddle straight up in the air."

Looking at the space between the seats and the floor of the raft, I know this command will be extremely difficult, fitting what is essentially the size of a baby elephant down in what is a fetal position, then hopping back up to paddle. While I was assessing this movement, Elmer issued more instructions which I now wish I had heard, like when you zone out on the plane and you suddenly hear the attendant say, "...put your arms through the straps and grasp the cushion to your chest."

Wait...what?

"If you fall out of the raft," Elmer says, "hold on to the rope on the side of the raft, and I will grab hold of your vest at the shoulders and pull you into the raft."

Did he say, fall out of the raft? I hadn't planned for that, I thought, pressing my helmet tighter to my head.

Although very fit, Elmer is two heads shorter than I, and I *know* I outweigh him even with all those spectacular tan muscles of his.

"Right," I laugh with a condescending smile, "I want to see you try that with *me*!"

The other passengers up front with Elmer lift up the raft and head down the embankment toward the water. I follow, whooping with excitement.

Elmer put me on the back right of the raft in front of him, and I pat myself on the back for having made it past the first hurdle, that of not falling into the water while stepping into the raft.

The first rapids come up quickly. Water splashes over the sides and front of the raft, baptizing our voyage. I hoot 'n holler as we bounce over the rippling water. We spin around a couple of times, go down backwards, and get caught up on the rocks.

Elmer gets out of the raft and pushes us off the rocks, then effortlessly hops back into the raft. In spite of those muscles, he could defy gravity. He paddle-slaps the river sending a wall of refreshing water onto us, soaking us to the skin, something the man from Chicago clearly hated. He hunched his shoulders and thrust his paddle in the air trying to ward off the shower, as if that would save him. I guess he forgot to splash on his *pura vida* this morning.

While we wait for the other rafts to catch up, Elmer collects plants from the river's edge and adorns each of our helmets. The other teams, also sporting various plants or flowers on their helmets, arrive and suddenly we became tribes, each raft seeking to outperform the others. As we sat, slowly drifting with the current of the river, I look up into the tops of the towering trees along the riverbanks hoping to see sloths or monkeys. I was so taken by the lush green foliage that it didn't matter if I saw any of those things. THIS forest is stunning; as opposed to the one I am sporting beneath my board shorts.

We pass over more rapids and come to a calm piece of the river.

"You can go swimming, if you want to," Elmer says. Without a second thought as to what might lie beneath the surface of the water, the Chicago woman and I go over the side of the raft and into the river. Lying back and floating along with the current releases such a delicious laziness in me. I am so thankful I put on a pair of shorts over my undergrowth since the Chicago woman has her perky taut body in a tiny little bikini with no sign of shrubbery. In contrast to her, without my shorts, one would have easily mistaken me for a howler monkey floating down the river.

One of the guides in a passing raft yelled, "Watch out for the Piranha!"

I shout back, "It's okay--they'll save me money on having to get liposuction!"

Elmer calls us to get back into the raft. I watch as he grasps the shoulder straps of the Chicago woman, a petite size six sort of gal, and hoists her onto the raft. He draws her out of the water in what appears to be a slow motion scene from a romantic movie, her pointed toes gingerly touching down onto the floor of the raft in full standing position. It was breathtaking.

Now it is my turn.

Elmer grabs hold of the shoulder straps of my vest to bring me back into the raft, but instead of the daintily performed spectacle from the moment before, I fly out of the water and land on top of him like a Goliath grouper, pinning Elmer to the bottom of the raft. The "grouper" with her feet dangling over the side of the raft, leaving her body positioned in a slightly arched Superman pose, cannot get any footing with which to pull herself up, and so I lie there, immobilized. Elmer, on the bottom of the raft being pinned by a woman twice his size, can only lay there helplessly laughing…and gasping for air.

"You know," I blurt out through breathless laughter, "I was hoping I would get laid on this trip, and I think this might be as close as I'm gonna get!"

The couple from Chicago broke into howls of laughter.

Once we regain our proper positions and dignity, we paddle off down the river. I see men standing alongside the left riverbank several yards ahead of us. I can't imagine why we would be meeting up with them as Elmer steers our raft over to the bank, but when we get there, the men begin handing over whole watermelons and pineapples. We load them onboard and push off again downstream.

Halfway down the river, we ground the raft at what appears to be a river beach spot. The guides flip over one of the rafts to be used as a table and pull knives out of their vests to carve up our load of fruit collected from the men alongside the river. Within seconds, they filet the fruit into an attractive display of bite-sized appetizers. Is this the best pineapple I have ever eaten, or is it just the setting?

After our snack and a stretch of our legs, we continue down the river energized from our pit stop, and bounce our way through another set of rapids. Once again, we come to a calm stretch of river and, once again, we go swimming. This time Elmer joins us, leaving the Chicago man alone in the raft. The water is invigorating since the day has heated up a bit and we are sweating under our life preservers and helmets.

Determined not to get pinned to the bottom of the raft again, Elmer, after getting himself back into the raft and daintily hoisting the Chicago woman aboard, comes over to me giving me the Stink Eye and says, "Now, this time, I want you to kick off when I say three!"

He grasps the shoulders on my vest, counts to three, and pulls. I kick as hard as I can, but I have forgotten Elmer's pre-flight instructions on re-tightening the straps on my vest once they get wet. The vest slides up over my arms and head, pinning my arms up in the air, stopping only by the last lowest strap so that now I can't breathe nor can I use my arms…and, I'm sinking back into the water! I hear Elmer making what can only be described as disparaging Tico expletives as he lies down on the side of the raft and starts grappling for the bottom of my vest to pull it back down, while simultaneously trying to find the straps to tighten them. Needless to say, some other items are grappled in the encounter, but I was too concerned about drowning to enjoy the experience.

Once situated back into my corset of life, barely able to breathe from the tension Elmer has put in the straps, he grasps my shoulder straps again, and with renewed adrenaline fueling his muscles, he pulls me out of the water, but flings me to the side avoiding the pinning he received earlier. I land on the floor of the raft, face down wedged between the seat and the stern with my legs resting up on the side of the raft resulting in that lovely Superman pose. The Goliath Grouper has landed once more.

Our journey ends all too soon for me, as we come aground just past an overhead bridge which spans the river. The guides point us up the steep embankment to the waiting vans with our bags of dry clothes and personal items. We had stashed them in the van prior to heading to the river.

A short bus ride takes us to a lovely pavilion where the BEST meal of my entire trip awaits, possibly because I am now starving. Our guides serve us a delicious hot meal complete with chayote that is to die for. During the meal, the photographer who had been snapping photos during our ride down the rapids, brings over small screens whereby we can view our pictures as we eat. The Chicago couple seated across from me didn't want to pay the small fee to buy their photos, but I eagerly purchase mine not knowing if I will ever experience a birthday trip quite like this one.

As I leave my seat to walk towards the back of the pavilion to pay, the twenty-something young photographer undresses me with his eyes and looks me up and down. No doubt, he was smitten with my dazzling beauty from the day's drenching.

I pause for a moment considering this sweet young photographer's interest. There is nothing unappealing about this man. I 'm just not attracted to him. Not like I am to Jon. Then I get a vision of the photographer running for his life from the howler monkey as I slip out of my shorts and give a derisory snort at the thought.

Perhaps it is the refreshing water or the stunning location or finally grasping the concept of *pura vida*, but I am suddenly aware of the great wave of acceptance that washed over me today, and I'm no longer worried about my body or the condition of my bikini area. I am embracing the fullness that life has to offer in this moment, the *pura vida*. It is a way of seeing life. I let go of my fears and failures today and experienced pure joy.

"Would you like to meet up with me later tonight?" the young photographer asks with a smooth, Spanish lilt in his voice.

"Thanks for the complement, but you would need a machete," I said walking away wearing my Dad's smirk.

Subsequent to my superlative white water rafting experience, I stop in at the hotel office before heading to my cabin.

"Oneida," I greet the young woman behind the desk. "Did you have any success getting me into the Maleku Village?"

"No, I so sorry. Construction on de road make it impossible to get there." She thought for a moment, then her face brightened with an idea. "Umm, wait, I know another place that might have de masks. Let me call." She quickly dials a number into the phone and speaks in Spanish. I hear "Si, si," a few times, so I'm guessing it might be good news.

"Yes, they have them," Oneida says hanging up the phone, "but, if you going to make it before they close, you must go now. You only have half hour."

"H-How will I get there?"

"No problem!" Oneida said, "I know just the person to call!"

In less than two minutes, a red taxi slides into the driveway of the hotel's office and a man frantically waves at me to get into the car. I pull open the passenger side door and instinctively reach for the seat belt. This is one of those times I did NOT want to forget that safety harness. The driver flies down the two-lane road at breakneck speed, passing and swerving around cars and trucks.

This is a TOTALLY insane taxi ride to get to *Ecocentro Danaus,* where I am to view the Maleku masks. If my life's bucket list included a ride in the Daytona 500, this surely would check it off. Looking like a spider straddling two walls, I slam my right foot up against the front floor board, my left foot presses against the center console of the car, and my right hand braces itself on the headliner, I grasp the right shoulder of the driver to let him know that I was not dying alone on this ride and try not to scream.

Astoundingly, we arrive in one piece. The driver parks and rushes me towards the entrance. With adrenaline still coursing through my veins, I look up and stop dead in my tracks. There in a low bough of a Cecropia tree in front of me at the edge of the parking lot, I see the Brown-throated three-toed sloth I lamented missing the night before. Only now I get to see it in the waning daylight and up close. He slowly chews on a leaf while regarding us with casual indifference as other visitors and I snap photos.

Sloths have such an adorable face with dark circles around their eyes that reach down to the cheeks. The circles meet up with the outer corners of their mouth making a permanent smile. They have a short, blunt snout that looks like a dog's nose. You just wanna cuddle them. But their fur is an ecosystem in and of itself, hosting no less than a hundred moths, fungi, algae, mites, and ticks. I think I'll fight back that emotional embrace. It's the dry season now so this little guy is currently brown. During the rainy season, four species of algae living on the sloth's fur turn green, both aiding in camouflage and making him an unappetizing meal.

Three-toed sloth. Check.

"Pura Vida!" I try to exclaim, but my *vida* is cut short as my driver pulls me quickly inside before closing time. A member of the Maleku on staff shows me to the Cultural House to see the masks. To the Maleku, each animal is imbued with certain aspects of their nature. They then carve these masks out of Balsa wood, some with just one animal, others with more intricate designs that tell a story. The blue butterfly represents peace and good luck. Macaws mate for life so they are always seen in twos

and represent fidelity. The Jaguar is a warrior representing strength, audacity and intelligence. The coral snake stands for healing powers, and the toucan for the inner beauty of a woman.

I follow the employee and enter the Cultural House where my mouth falls open at the number of masks adorning the walls — all for sale. And they take credit cards!

Lost in the beauty and meaning of the artwork before me, I can't decide which ones to buy. Apparently, the selection process is taking longer than I realize because the taxi driver bursts onto the scene shouting orders at the poor Maleku employee who is waiting patiently for me to make up my mind and pay. I quickly select my masks: a Blue Morpho butterfly, a Jaguar, two Scarlet Macaws, and a mask that tells the story of the eruption of Arenal Volcano in 2010. My driver sweeps up the packages and hastily moves me along the path back to the taxi where, again, I brace myself for a harrowing Tico NASCAR run back to the hotel.

I wonder what animal the Maleku would carve into a mask to represent this driver.

Maleku Masks.

MONTEVERDE

In the early morning hours, a light mist baptizes the crossing of Lake Arenal from La Fortuna to Monteverde as the pontoon boat sails off into low ethereal clouds. I feel like I'm in a scene from the movie, *The Lord of the Rings*.

The boat is fitted with rows of white fiberglass bench seats and open sides. Rolled up and tied with black Velcro straps are clear plastic "windows" that can be rolled down in inclement weather, which today's drizzle apparently doesn't qualify. Above the rolled up windows runs a metal rack that holds life preservers, hopefully unneeded. The water is dark grey-green reflecting the cloud cover overhead.

I try striking up a conversation with a solo traveler seated in front of me, but her short, clipped answers sideways over her shoulder tells me she wants to be left alone. The other travelers have seated themselves all the way in the back of the boat and speaking a language that may be Gaelic for all I know. I'm fine alone and settle into a dreamy observation of the scenery.

My father would have loved this. As far back as I can remember, my dad always had some sort of floating vessel. He loved fishing and being out on the water, even though he couldn't swim.

Neither of my parents could swim, which looking back on it from an adult perspective, is a tragedy since I was part fish. Perhaps they felt a pang of responsibility should I start to drown because one summer, they both took adult swimming lessons. I, of course, went along to provide pointers. Apparently, I was excellent at this because the instructor kept saying, "That's good, now go away."

My mother being 5'10" tall in the three foot section of the pool knew all she had to do was stand up to keep from drowning, but she had a major phobia of water. Simply splashing her in the face evoked panic breathing and wailing. She never learned to swim.

My father was not afraid of the water. He just had zero buoyancy. He literally sank like a rock. When I would go over to the edge of the pool to give him pointers, he would be lying flat on the bottom of the pool with his arms and legs kicking and waving, but going nowhere. The only way he could make any headway would be to crawl along the bottom of the pool like a lobster. He never learned to swim.

I, however, learned to water ski, drive the boat, trailer the boat, and, of course fish, all on my father's small vessels. He even had a pontoon boat like the one I'm on now. I crunch forward as a pang of longing for him grips my stomach.

We move along the choppy water with the steel-blue mountains in the distance, their tops obscured by clouds. Slowly, out of the mist and clouds, a small, green island covered in lush undergrowth and dotted with trees appears off the port bow. I imagine a quaint, humble dwelling of stone sitting on the island with smoke curling out of its chimney from the wood-burning stove inside. I day dream of my little island home with its solitude and fairytale critters running around like a scene out of *Snow White* until I can no longer see it as the clouds once again envelop the island into obscurity. Since it is uninhabited, naturally, I claim it for my own, and dub it *"Brigadoon."* I feel the name suitable for my tiny disappearing island.

I am just about to drift off into a lovely fantasy involving Jon, my tiny island habitat, and a hand-carved canopy bed when the boat comes ashore on the opposite side of the lake where a couple of men are assisting with the docking and a handful of adolescent Tico boys wait eagerly to take our bags. Since I had been warned to keep close tabs on my belongings, my first instinct is to tell them "NO." But, I look past them to the steep slippery, muddy climb up a hill to reach the waiting bus, and I mellow a bit on my decision. I hand the bags over to a slightly chubby boy, figuring he'd be easier to catch should he take off with my bags.

After much assistance in scaling the muddy slope, I follow the child as he rounds the rear of the bus and hands off my luggage to a man who shoves them into the back of the vehicle. The boy's eyes grow as wide as his smile as I tip him five dollars, and he runs off to show his friends. I think about tipping the three men who aided me in getting up the hill, but feel fairly certain there isn't enough cash in my backpack to cover that action.

I find a window seat on the bus, keeping my backpack on my lap. You don't have to tell me twice! The views of the mountainside from the small bus are breathtaking. I wonder if the locals tire of seeing so much green rolled out along the hills like yards of verdant velvet heaped up on a cutting table in Jo-Ann's Fabrics.

At the top of what I think is the highest mountain peak, large concrete pillars arise out of the earth in the middle of nowhere. The bus window won't allow me to see the top of the pillars, so I scrunch down on the floor in the same position I had experienced while white water rafting to see what secrets these pillars hold.

Huge metal arms are atop the concrete poles. It's a field of giant metal windmills on both sides of our bus, turning steadily in the breeze like a cluster of children's plastic pinwheels. Their large metal blades scoop at the sky as they slowly rotate, generating power. I remember the article I had read on one of Costa Rica's environmental choices. For the past several decades, 93% or more of Costa Rica's electricity has come from renewable resources, like harnessing the wind up here on the mountains.

What an ecologically brilliant use of natural assets! However, I feel a colorful paint job with spiral stripes on the concrete columns would give it a *Willie Wonka* feel and spruce up the sight.

The sun glints off the blades of the windmills and I catch a glimpse of *Don Quixote* out of the corner of my mind, valiantly tilting at these metallic giants with sword raised to strike in the name of his beloved Dulcinea. For once, I don't cast myself in the role of helpless heroine in need of rescuing, but I am on horseback alongside of him, unsteadily charging at the giants in my life, real or imagined, but charging nonetheless.

Our bus enters the little town of Santa Elena and begins dropping off tourists at hotels along the main road. My hotel is on the outskirts of town so I am the last to be deposited.

"Hotel Montana de Monteverde," announces the driver. I look out the window and look down to see a lodge sitting on a ledge of Santa Elena just hanging there off the side of a mountain. I'll never understand how these buildings don't just roll down the mountain and off a cliff. The hotel itself looks more like something you would encounter in a ski area out west in the U.S. It's made of a golden shade of some kind of wood in the style of a chalet with an A-line roof. Although the hotel looks small from this perspective, I have to remember we are on a road higher than the roof line.

Are you really going to make me walk down this gravel driveway to get to the front door?

"I take you to de front door, don't worry!" he says.

Did I say that out loud?

I can just see me sliding on my ass down that gravely steep slope.

The driver takes out my bags once we reach the entrance, and I thank him for his assistance. I enter through the towering glass front doors to an impressive lobby with soaring cathedral ceilings of exposed wood. Straight through the lobby to the back of the hotel, I can see the mountains through a wall of windows. All along the back of the hotel runs a wide covered veranda where I see guests seated at tables drinking in the stunning view. Maybe they're having an iced tea smoothie.

"Welcome to Hotel Montana de Monteverde," a woman called out to me from the desk against the wall to my right, "Do you have reservation?"

"Yes, let me get out my confirmation for you."

"No need. Just tell me your name."

God, I love efficiency.

A smiling young man, probably the same age as Jon, but missing the turn on-factor, hoists my bags over his shoulders and leads me to my room down a very steep concrete walkway with intermittent small landings between the flights of steps.

I better remember this slope if I try this climb after drinking.

My accommodations do not disappoint. As the door opens to my room, I'm met with an exquisite view right off my patio. In the distance, over the top of the mountains, I can see the Gulf of Nicoya, an extension of the Pacific Ocean. I collect my chin from off the floor and roll in my tongue. Directly off my patio is about twenty feet or so of thick green grass that then gives way to a rocky drop off. The ground continues rolling down the side of the mountain to a small garden pond surrounded by flowering plants. The room has a vaulted ceiling with open beams similar to the foyer, two standard queen beds, and a typical desk.

But it is the bathroom that gets the, "Oh, wow!" factor.

It is roughly the size of my second bedroom back in the states. There is a wainscoting of decorative tile all around from the double sink vanity past the tub and back again. Walls are tiled up to the vaulted ceiling, where a large skylight pours sunshine over a HUGE forest green spa tub complete with jets and a hand-held shower wand. You can fit a party in that tub.

Hell with that! I can fit Jon and me in that tub.

I dig my phone out of my backpack. Hey, there's service! Quickly, I punch in his phone number and wait. No answer. No voice mail. Damn it. I shove the phone back in my backpack along with some other things I will need for today's excursions.

The downside, and I mean down, to my room is that it's virtually straight down the side of the mountain from the main veranda. It isn't the going TO the room that presents an issue — unless you're drunk. In fact, if I had leg muscles like a gazelle and could leap from the top of the hill, I might possibly land on the roof of my room. It's the coming UP those flights of stairs and angled concrete pathways from the room that would make the Stair Master equipment at the gym weep with envy. Believe me, you only want to do this trek once a day.

The brilliant green hillsides of Monteverde are a fitting intro to the plethora of things to do here. This is where I will celebrate my actual birthday, and I'm filled with excitement. I toss my bags onto the dresser and take off huffing and puffing my way back up the path to find something to eat. I would stay and daydream about a roaring good time in that tub and not torture my quadriceps, but I'm starving. My stomach always wins out. Besides, I'm actually looking forward to scrambled eggs, rice and beans.

JOHN WAYNE, QUAKERS, AND POO

The next day's adventures begin with a hike in the *Children's Eternal Rain Forest* a short distance from the hotel, so I walk. From my trusty *Fodor's* guide to Costa Rica, I know that a teacher from Sweden, worried about the unprotected forest around Monteverde, started this reserve. She and her students raised the funds themselves. Since the initial reserve was created, thousands of hectares have been added by other philanthropic organizations internationally.

The day is sunny, dry, and hot. Not what I expect from a rainforest. I enter the reserve and begin following the dusty path, grumbling with dissatisfaction.

"I can see a forest like this back in Florida anytime I want. I'm sweating bullets in this heat. I didn't think I would need sunscreen in a rainforest. Why did I spend all this money to come see the same thing I can see..."

BAM! In the instant that gripe passes across my mind, I find myself flat on my ass, and I don't mean a donkey. Falling definitely does not happen in slow motion from multiple angles like it does in the movies. One minute I am standing and in the next blink of my eye, I'm on the ground. I sit, bewildered, assessing all of my body parts for broken bones, and sure enough, something was broken—the viewing screen on my new camera cracked under my donkey when I landed on it.

God, forgive me for complaining, I prayed silently like a penitent child. I drag myself up off the ground to resume my trek along the path, repentant for my ungrateful thoughts.

As I trek along the dusty path of the *Children's Eternal Rain Forest,* black squirrels race through the trees above my head, down the trunks, and across a low branch passing directly in front of me. I would have hit my head on the branch had it not been for them scurrying right past my nose. I resist the urge to scream, "SQUIRREL!!" in true Chevy Chase's *Christmas Vacation* form, but I am not sure how that might translate into Spanish. My luck, it would be something akin to screaming "BOMB" in an airport, and I would be detained for further questioning.

Close to the end of the trail, I come to a fork in the path. One way appears to be the exit, but I am not certain of the other direction. At that moment, I hear noise coming from the exit path. Supposing it to be another hiker, I turn to ask if this is the way out, but come face-to-knee with a White Nose Coati — Check — a cousin of the raccoon. I know it is a male because he is alone, strutting down the path with a Jon Wayne swagger. The females hang together as a group; sipping drinks at Starbucks and male Coati bashing, I imagine. He seems neither threatened nor impressed with my presence as I fumble to get the camera out of my pocket, but not before the Coati meanders off the path, disappearing into the foliage.

Dammit to hell! What is your problem? Have your camera ready, woman!

As I exit *The Children's Eternal Rainforest* on my way to the Cheese Factory, I follow a narrow path that is elevated above the street by a healthy 10 to 15 feet. A lifesaver, as I see it, given the driving habits of the Tico taxi drivers.

I review the critters I still want to see here in Costa Rica, one of which being the stunningly beautiful blue butterfly. As God is my witness, the second that thought passes through my mind, a Blue Morpho Butterfly flutters out of the forest from the opposite side of the road, dances above the speeding taxis and flies over to my side of the street. It flutters inches from my face, hanging suspended in the air before disappearing into the forest behind me.

"Now you're just showing off, God. Dammit! I missed the

picture again!"

Morpho Butterfly. Check.

I walk toward my next adventure at the Cheese Factory, storing the missed photos on the memory card of my mind.

The dust and the heat are making me sluggish, so I thought a good cup of hot coffee would do me right about then. I stop in at a little bakery alongside the road and pick up a large cupcake to use as my birthday cake and ask the woman behind the counter for a cup of coffee.

"No café," she said.

"Is there somewhere around here where I can get a cup of coffee?"

She tips her head to the right and raises her left eyebrow looking at me with the, "Really?" eyes gesturing out the window of the front of the store. I turn to see what she is trying to show me. There across the street sits an actual twenty-foot wide, cream-color teacup and saucer in front of a coffee shop.

Duh.

Suspecting that the bakery lady has probably called the coffee shop woman to tell her a stupid American was heading her way, I skip the coffee shop. The embarrassment would be too much for me to swallow right now, so I walk on towards the Cheese Factory.

"I'm sorry, ma'am, but you've just missed the last tour of the Cheese Factory for the day," said the young man standing at the entrance wearing black pants and a white shirt with the sleeves rolled up.

"What? Dude, you've got to be kidding me! I have just hiked here in the heat. I'm sweaty, hungry, and I want something cold to drink that's not water," I growled.

"The store is open. You can take care of all of those problems just by going through this door," he says as he opens the door for me, undaunted by my surly behavior.

"Okay, then, I'll just have myself a party sampling the different cheeses, thank you."

Wrong again.

What is it they say? "When you assume, you make an ass out of U and Me." I *assumed* that this was a place where I could sample some local cheeses for lunch like it said on the Internet, but instead you have to buy a whole block of cheese, not just samples.

I am hungry, it's lunchtime, and by God, I'm going to eat some cheese.

After much deliberation, I settle upon the smallest hunk of cheese I can find and sit down at one of the bistro tables to partake of its creamy deliciousness. While I gorge myself on the block of cheese, one of the workers gives me a pasteurized version of the factory's history.

"It all started with four pacifist Quakers from Alabama being incarcerated for several years after refusing to enter the draft for the Korean War. When they got out, they sought a country where they could live in peace," he says.

"You know, when I first learned of a cheese factory in Monteverde," I say with cheeks full of cheese like a squirrel hoarding nuts, "I thought this an odd place to put a factory. Why Costa Rica?"

"Costa Rica attracted the Friends mainly because it doesn't have an army. The country did away with their military in 1948 when the government came up with the idea of diverting the money spent on the army to spending it on health and education."

I take a drink and consider what that might cost the country in security.

"In 1951," my Gouda-friend continues, "eleven families of

Quakers came from Alabama to Costa Rica's green, cool climate and found it perfect for dairy farming. They're the ones who gave Monteverde its name, meaning 'green mountain' in Spanish."

"Well, the name's appropriate, but I can't quite get on board with that "cool climate" comment. Do you see me sitting here with dried sweat crystals on my clothes?"

He blinks at me. "San Jose is much warmer than it is here. Perhaps it will cool off a bit tomorrow.

"Thanks to the Quakers' desire to live a more peaceful life," he continues unaffected by my potential to self-combust, "more than 46,000 acres have been set aside to protect a diverse array of flora and fauna."

"That's an amazing story. Thank you for sharing it with me," I say. "But I've one question. How long did it take to get the cows to grow two of their legs shorter than the others so they could stand on the steep slopes?"

Nothing. Just a deadpan look of incomprehension crossed his face. There's just no getting a smile out of this guy. I guess you don't grow much of a sense of humor standing around watching cheese age.

I finish my unorthodox lunch with a scoop of Macadamia ice cream and walk along the dirt road toward my next destination, the *Bat Jungle*.

Jon hasn't called back. I look at my phone. No service. How do people communicate up here?

You're a fool, you know that? He's probably having a good laugh with his friends about how he played you. You're so gullible.

Great. A scoop of self-flagellation to top off my ice cream cone.

Halfway to the *Bat Jungle*, I pass a uniquely shaped building and stop to investigate. It's the local artisans' boutique, a hand-carved octagon-shaped gazebo. A piece of art itself. The

113

walls are either actual tree limbs or they have been carved to appear as such. Glass is fitted along the inside of the branch walls so the shop can be air conditioned, something I am welcoming right about now.

I step inside to browse the products on the shelves, anxious to find some locally made treasures to take home. But I'm disappointed to find that most of the goods have tags from Guatemala and aren't made in Costa Rica.

Close, but no cigar. I purchase a simple pair of wood and wire earrings that are actually made by a local artist, and leave.

Back on the road to the bat cave, sweat dripping in uncomfortable places along with my rapidly melting ice cream cone, I reach the door to the attraction. From the moment I enter the museum, a wave of nostalgia washes over me — as well as AC.

I stand in the doorway breathing a huge groan of relief from the heat outside while gasping at the posters and books all around me.

The attendant behind the desk must've thought I was having some sort of cardiac event because he stands up wide-eyed and asked, "Ma' me, are you alright?"

"Fine," I managed to croak out in between gasps.

"When my son, Child #3, was six years old, he was absorbed in learning everything about bats. Being in here is like…like I've just stepped back in time," I say looking around the room. "He was mesmerized by the comic book character, Batman. It didn't matter whether it was Michael Keaton or Val Kilmer behind the cowl, just as long as the guy had on the costume."

"Oh, well, we don't have Batman stuff here," he said raising one eyebrow at me as he sat back down.

As I peruse the room, I see the same materials I used twenty years ago in teaching my children and bat house kits from the same conservancy that had supplied the materials for the one my son used decades ago. Merlin Tuttle, founder of Bat Conservation International in 1982 and Merlin Tuttle's Bat Conservation, took the majority of bat photos in magazines and posters. Tuttle wanted to set the record straight on bats by providing factual information about them and their habitats. These teaching tools have stood the test of time, continuing to educate the public on the importance of bats.

Nearly every day in 1996, my son would dress in a Batman mask, cape, Batman tighty-whities—and cowboy boots. Always cowboy boots.

Since I homeschooled my children then, I needed to keep him busy in the room with the girls and me, so I gave him bat paperwork, books, and games. He eagerly soaked up every fact on bats I put in front of him, all the while wearing his Batman outfit.

While preparing schoolwork for my son, I flipped through a copy of *Bat Conservation International* magazine—the same publications they have here at the *Bat Jungle* twenty-three years later—I ran across an article on a biologist who studied a colony of bats that had taken up residency in a condo building in the Florida Keys.

Road Trip! I packed up the baby and grabbed the young ladies and off we went to the Keys to meet with this biologist. He was more than thrilled to talk bats with my children.

We arrived at the State of Florida Agriculture field office in the Keys a few hours before dusk. A quilted wall hanging, designed from one of Child #3's drawings, was presented to the biologist. My son had stitched it together while sitting on my lap at our sewing machine.

"This is really beautiful," he said, looking at my son. "You made this?"

"I drew it and then my mom made a pattern and then I cut it out," my son puffed out his chest.

"Then your mom sewed it together?"

"No! I sewed it on the sewing machine myself," Child #3 responded slightly indignant.

"Oh! Forgive me," said the biologist. "Can you tell me the story of what's happening in the picture?"

My son, seemingly convinced he was dealing with an ignorant grownup who obviously knew nothing about bats or art, set about describing his creation with a roll of his eyes and a sigh.

"Well, bats only come out at night. See the moon? And some sleep upside down in trees, so that's here. And some live in caves. That's what this is and those are bats coming out of the cave and this is the fruit some of them eat. This was all in my 4-H speech," said my son satisfied with his demonstration but slightly annoyed that the man had missed his speech.

Seeing that he was being schooled by a six year old, the doctor stepped up his game. He took us into the lab where he was preparing a dead bat to be sent to Tallahassee as a sample for research.

"Okay, everybody put on these gloves so we can keep germs to a minimum," he said handing us all medical gloves.

"I want to show you the wings. I'm going to gently unfold this bat's wing so you can see it better. A bat's wing is actually a lot like your hand. See how it moves?" He showed the children how the wings open and move in flight then let them hold the bat and unfold the wings themselves.

"The wing bones, here, are elongated fingers, and this little claw is the thumb. Bats' fingers are long so they can support the width of the wing. The wing is made up of material similar to the tiny flaps of skin joining the bases of your fingers." The children looked at their hands through the opaque medical gloves, but saw nothing.

The biologist then turned his attention to the ears. "Bats actually use their ears to "see" through a process known as—"

"Echolocation," shouted the children like contestants on *Family Feud.*

"Wow, you guys really know your stuff," he said. "See how big the ears are compared to its body? That makes it easier to get information about its surroundings and to find its food. These folds in the ears help to capture sounds just like the shape of the nose picks up sound waves to locate insects."

With rubber gloves and a syringe in hand, the biologist said to my son, "So, are you ready to help me preserve this bat?"

"Yes!"

With what seemed like the skilled hands of a trained nurse, my son, guided by the scientist, inserted the syringe exactly how the biologist instructed and pushed the plunger to fill the bat with formaldehyde.

The girls watched wide-eyed. "Cool," they cooed in unison.

I succeeded in suppressing a repulsive exclamation of "GROSS!"

"The next thing to do before sending this little guy to Tallahassee for research is add your name to the official label on the jar," said the biologist. "Tell me how to spell your name."

"It starts with an 'A,'" my son directed. They finished filling out the label for the jar listing my son as the assistant in pickling the mammal. Somewhere in Tallahassee is a bat with my son's name on it.

Na-na-na-na-na-na-na-na, Batman!

After the preservation of the bat, it was approaching dusk,

so the biologist led us on a short drive to the community to witness the bats as they emerged from their roost.

"Now, are you sure you're not going to get scared when the bats start flying," he asked. "They will swoop down and fly circles around you, but don't be afraid. They won't hurt you nor will they roost in your hair," he said debunking a popular myth we knew to be a tall tale.

We waited.

And waited.

Nothing. I was just about to pack it in when I began hearing clicks in the dark, first in my right ear, then left. The bats. So small and fast we could barely make them out as they flew past us, mapping their surroundings with sonar-like clicks. The children squealed with excitement as the sounds got louder and bats swooped through the air around us.

The clicking. Clicking. It's so loud...

I shook myself out of my memory and realized the clicking was coming from a speaker over my head. I looked around to see if anybody was watching my temporary lapse of reality, but they were all engrossed in the displays.

I'm standing by a wall display decreeing the superior quality of bat guano, errr....bat poo, as it differs from other types of natural fertilizer. Bat guano has a higher concentration of nutrients than other poos, according to poo experts.

Entering into the bat cave, the lights are low and red so as not to not disturb the bats, but still provide enough for quality viewing. Approximately ninety bats and eight species reside at the *Bat Jungle*, and you can hear them behind the protective glass by way of special headphones.

This man-made habitat allows humans to observe bats, but, just as in old zoos, it doesn't give the bats much freedom. I understand the complexities involved studying bats in a natural

118

habitat. I hope one day scientists might conceive an arboretum style to allow space for them to fly, while still providing opportunity to appreciate these amazing mammals.

As I watch the bats behind the protective glass, a rush of satisfaction swells within me. I realize I had done a good job teaching my children. Giving myself kudos has not always been something I'm comfortable with. I seldom feel like I am enough in attaining tasks in my life, but at this moment, I feel pride in the job I had done with homeschooling.

I finish my ice cream and a few bats behind the glass join me in eating pieces of fruit—except they're eating theirs upside down. A trick I refuse to try.

Standing in the near dark, my inner child slaps me upside the head with a memory of another encounter I had with a bat long before my son presented an interest in them, sending me back to when I was a child of about two years of age and my brother was around six.

For whatever reason, my family was living in an attic. Who knows why? A bat was flurrying around the attic trying to escape the glowing bare light bulb dangling from the center of the ceiling. My mother, Wilma, was screaming in terror. Our father yelled to my brother and me to pull the bed sheet over our heads.

Not wanting to miss out on the excitement and the sheet being threadbare, I peered at my father jumping from bed to bed in his boxer shorts and socks. He was holding a broom in his hands as he chased the bat trying to kill it, swinging like Babe Ruth, and cussing like a sailor.

"Goddammit! Come back here, you sonofabitch! Wilma, shut the hell up! You two keep that sheet over your heads. Dammit! You ferughkyuhing thing," our father gurgled in an attempt to curtail his cursing.

My brother and I don't remember the outcome of the Great Bat Battle, but what we have realized is that our father handled most emergencies in his underwear and socks.

"Can 'ya move, please?" It's the stinky old man sitting next to me on the flight home. His finger pokes me hard in the shoulder. "I need to go!"

"Oh, of course! I'm so sorry," I stammer. I was deep in thought and didn't hear him. I fight to free myself from the seat belt and stand, but as I turn to move into the aisle, I run smack into the flight attendant's beverage cart. Instantly, my closet claustrophobia flares up like a startled Grizzly bear in spring and my heart starts racing.

"Move it," I roar to the attendant, "this guy has an emergency!" My face must look like that crazed Grizzly because she releases the brake on the cart and pulls it backward—only to crash into the other cart directly behind her. Panic at the blocked intersection makes me leap like a gazelle onto my seat. Then I spring over the armrest, landing in the aisle in front of the cart in search of a large enough space where I can breathe and calm down.

Oh, my God, I'm trapped in a tin can thousands of feet in the air! Hold on. Calm down. Stay calm or they'll tie you up and drop you in Mexico to walk home.

The carts, the flight attendants, and the rolling cans of spilled soda left the aisle clogged like the arteries of a bacon-loving swamp monster, and there was no escape. The old man's bowels explode where he stands, filling the cabin with a pungent "Ode de Sewer" scent. Groans of disgust and gagging sounds erupt throughout the plane as people reach for their airsickness bags, of which there are none. Claustrophobia is my friend for

120

once as it removed me from my seat just in the nick of time before the man ripened his pants.

I'm not concerned about the tightness of the cabin now.

Give me bat guano. That smell's not half as bad as this. Focus on Jon. Focus on Jon. I keep repeating my mantra as I slump into an empty seat in the back of the plane. I closed my eyes, pinched my nose closed with my pinkie fingers and plugged my ears with my ring fingers. La-la-la-la-la-la-la.

What a stark contrast to my flight to Costa Rica with Jon by my side.

One of the goals on this trip was to stay in a tree house hotel, but they'd been booked up a year in advance. The next best thing would be to have dinner in one. I know that there's a tree house restaurant in Santa Elena. Dinner in a tree house would have to suffice.

I trudge toward the center of town and the restaurant.

"Uno," I say to the hostess as I reach the tree house and hold up my index finger. She leads me into a dining area around the base of the monster-sized tree then up a flight of stairs to the second "floor" amongst the tree limbs to a small table overlooking the mountainside. Overhead is another floor encircling the tree. All along the tree trunk, limbs, and railings are strung small white lights, glittering like little woodland fairies dancing in the breeze of the late afternoon wind. Dinner is an outstanding experience while sitting high in the boughs of a living tree. I can only imagine spending the night in a tree house.

Maybe Jon can join me? I look at my phone to see if I have service. I do!

I push the number to call Jon. My heart is pounding in my chest as I hear it ring. And ring. No answer.

Grrrrrrr, why isn't this man answering his phone? Now I'm pissed and I don't even want him here to share dinner.

You're such a liar.

Captivating smells waft up from the kitchen causing my mouth to water. I treat myself to a delicious steak, secretly thankful for the reprieve from scrambled eggs, rice and beans. I wash the guilt down with a lovely red wine.

Leaving the beautiful tree house, I make my way back to *Hotel Montana* and decide to catch the sunset on the veranda.

A waiter approaches from inside. "May I get you something to drink, ma' me?"

"Yes, can you bring me one of those frozen fruity drinks made with Cacique?"

"Yes, of course, ma'me," and scoots off inside.

Numerous hummingbird feeders have been hung all along the expansive porch looking out towards the ocean in the distance.

The waiter shows up with my drink.

Nature's little helicopters routinely make their way to the bird feeders, hovering just a foot or two away from me. I've never been this close to hummingbirds before, and I am lost in observing their iridescent colors and behaviors, passing away the time sipping my drink.

The alert on my phone goes off.

Jon! No, not Jon. *Dammit.*

The night hike. Holy crap, I'm gonna be late!

I leap up from my chair on the veranda, slog down my drink and get brain freeze, grab my backpack, throw a few dollars on the table, and head for the front entrance of the hotel where the transport van is just about to leave for the hike. The van is loaded already with adventurers, and I get the only seat left, riding shotgun. *Yay me!* It is too dark to read my Spanish cheat book, so the driver and I ride along in silence.

We "de-van" at a building; half looking like it could be an auto parts store and the other half a prison cellblock, a plain concrete room with no windows. I am the very last to pay for my hike, and we're told to wait a few minutes. With all of the chairs being taken, I remain standing next to the desk.

The cashier, sensing his job is completed, takes out an adult coloring book and colored pencils and continues to work on a previously colored page. Within the past few years, coloring is being touted as a great tool for stress relief.

What the hell is there to be stressed about in the rainforest?

We're directed outside and handed flashlights then they divide us into groups, assigning each group a guide.

With this army of people tramping through the forest, it certainly won't be like the quiet, personal hike I had in La Fortuna where we could hear each movement of the leaves and I could ask all the questions I wanted.

The first few groups head out into the forest, flashlights on. My group goes last, and I can't be more grateful. As each group files off into the forest darkness along various pathways, the mountainside illuminates with little dots of yellow light looking like hundreds of fireflies in an Ohio yard on a summer evening.

Hello? Come back to the party, girl. Everybody else is walking away and the guide is talking about something.

"This is an Orange-bellied Trogon," our guide is saying as I catch up with the group. He shines his light on a branch where a bird is perched not far off the trail. I quickly dig out my critter field guide. A horizontal line of white feathers above its orange belly separates the green head of this 10-inch long bird making him look like he's wearing a golf shirt.

"Over there in those trees, are two Keel-billed Toucans aka

the Rainbow-billed Toucans," the guide shines his light on them. These toucans are different from the ones I saw in La Fortuna with different colors on their bills, but these guys aren't any happier about being disturbed from their slumber than their predecessors.

I have a sudden craving for Fruit Loops.

"These toucans have oversized bills that can grow to be a third of the size of the toucan's 20-inch body."

How do they keep from tipping over? I'm reminded of women wearing bouffant hairstyles in the sixties in six-inch heels. Now, there was a balancing act to rival the toucans.

We march along single file through the forest, and I can't help but think that, from high above, we must look like the trail of leaf cutter ants I encountered on the first night hike in La Fortuna.

I'm introduced to several amphibians as we stop alongside a stream. A red-eyed stream frog. A Brilliant frog, and some other type of female frog with a hump on her back for the male to hang onto when mating. I know I'll never look at a hunched-back woman in quite the same way again. I push back my shoulders and straighten my posture.

With all of these frogs, it's hard to imagine that the amphibian population has been taking a nosedive all over the world. It's thought that their population is a barometer of environmental health, like the canary in the coalmine trick.

The guide walks on a few steps more then stops.

"Here in its natural surroundings is a large black Tarantula," he says. We all tense up and take a step in various directions not sure where the arachnid is crouching. Turns out, it is hiding under leaves inside a tree stump next to my knees. The guide slowly moves aside the leaves, and I lean in for a photo op.

"Some species can throw urticating hairs with barbs from

their abdomens when they feel threatened," the guide cautions.

Now I know why the cashier was coloring.

"I'll get a picture online, thanks," I mumble, backing away.

You know what though…that could have been a cool design of human pubic hair. You wouldn't have to shave it or wax it. Just get pissed off and your problem is solved, in more ways than one. Population kept to a minimum, and I'd betcha rape statistics would fall, too.

"Look! On that branch," I ask pointing my flashlight on a limb several yards away. "What is that?"

"That's an Olingo," says Diego our guide. "We're very lucky to see him. He only comes out at night and is very shy."

"Shy? With all the racket he's making?" I suppose he can't help it, though. His banded tail is longer than a 360° Extendable Handle Swiffer Duster and twice as bushy. His fur is drab brown with cartoonish large, brown eyes.

"The better to see you with, my dear."

This Olingo is wise to keep a safe distance from me. Back in the United States, I have an unhealthy reputation with small bushy mammals.

I was doing a solo hike around the rim of Conkle's Hollow Nature Preserve in Hocking Hills State Park, Ohio. The rim is about 300 feet above the cool gorge floor. Getting hungry, I reached into my backpack for my apple and water, but they weren't there. That's when I remember I left them sitting on the front porch of the cabin I had rented.

Hummm, I'm more than halfway around the rim of this gorge, so the shorter distance back to food would be to continue going forward to get out. I folded up the map — sorta — stuffed it back in my pack and hastened my steps towards the exit.

125

Conkle's Hollow has two hiking trails. One that goes around the rim of the gorge with a three-hundred-foot drop down to the second trail which goes through the bottom of the gorge surrounded by a waterfall, cliffs, trees, and ferns. I had chosen to take the rim hike in the morning while the temperature was cooler. I could take the gorge path later in the day because it always stays cool down there.

Unfortunately, in my haste to get back to the cabin, one of my 11-sized feet got caught on a tree root hiding under the fall leaves, propelling me forward onto my face towards the edge of the cliff. I land with my arms outstretched in front of me, the edge of the rim only about two feet beyond my fingertips.

My splayed-out landing revealed more hidden by leaves than a tree root. It disrupted the hiding spot for a chipmunk. His head popped up from under the leaves, eyeball to eyeball with me. I saw terror in his beady little eyes as he looked right at me and I saw it spread across his little munk face as he leaped straight up out of the leaves to escape. Somehow, he turned direction in midair, and with all appendages spread out wide, he sailed over the edge of the cliff. I guess he forgot about the precipice he was perched upon.

"Nooooo!"

I crawled forward and peered over the edge catching sight of him clinging to a branch growing out of the wall of the cliff.

I frowned and said, "Sorry, little buddy."

I made it back to the cabin without further incident, but kept wondering why I'm so out of tune with nature when I love it so dearly. That, however, was not the worst of my encounters with wild furry critters.

It was 1972 and I was on my way to freedom.

Like every other teenager at that time, my rite of passage into adulthood was set in motion by the scheduling of my driver's test on my birthday.

"Mom! Let's go! I don't wanna be late for my appointment," I yelled as I stomped down the stairs and out to the car.

"I'm coming," she replied pulling the house door shut. "It would be nice if you were this punctual for school each morning. Give me the car keys. I'm driving."

"No! How will that look, showing up for my Driver's License test and me in the passenger seat? Besides, I've already got the seat and mirrors adjusted for me."

Huffing but giving in to my argument, Mom went around the car and got in on the passenger side, shutting her door.

"Go down here to the stop sign and turn left, then make a right and go down Allen Street," she directed.

"Mom, I know how to get to get there. Remember, I was there to get my learner's permit," I said with my nose in the air.

I pulled up at the DMV, careful to avoid my nemesis, parallel parking. Dad had tried relentlessly to teach me how to do it, and it just wouldn't stick, except for the tires, which would always stick to the curb because of something I did wrong when trying to parallel park.

Shedding Mom in the waiting room, I went into the test center for the written portion of the exam. I finished the test before everyone else and was sent on to do the driving portion. My instructor greeted me without a smile and grunted, "Uhm" as we left the building and got into my mom's car. He watched me as I put my foot on the brake pedal and started the car.

"Now I want you to go down to that light and make a right hand turn," he said, making notes on the form on his clipboard. He sent me through my paces, driving all around town, through the park, and over the railroad tracks.

"Okay, you're doing great. Let's do the parallel parking

and we'll be through," he breathed a sigh of relief.

I wanted to vomit.

I approached the cordoned off parking space. Once. Twice. I started to cry and so did the heavens. The sky opened up and dumped buckets of rain down on us.

To my total amazement, the instructor got out of the car in the deluge.

"I'm gonna help you a bit. Pull up there and let's do it again."

You only get three tries.

With the help of a now soaked instructor, I got the station wagon into that spot. What a feeling of accomplishment that was and not a shabby sixteenth birthday present either!

"I passed?"

The soggy instructor nodded his head.

"I PASSED! YES!" I screamed.

I dropped my mother back at the house and drove the wagon to gather up my posse for a cruise through town. I took them on the exact course I had driven with the instructor so they could all practice the route. I had turned sixteen first. I was riding cruising in style around the small road at the top of the city park, when suddenly, a chipmunk darted out from the shrubbery and ran under the front wheel of the driver side. There was no time to react. Thump!

I stopped the car to see if by some miracle he was alive, but he was dead.

"MURDERER! YOU KILLED IT!" the girls wailed.

We all began to cry and a couple of them suggested we give him a proper burial, but then none of us wanted to touch his dead body, so we just got back in the car and I drove them all home in silence

I was a murderer. Of tiny woodland creatures. I tried not

to think of myself in that light or the incident, but when my father got home from work, he reminded me of an instruction he had given me. He said, "What do you do if you're driving and an animal runs out in front of your car and you can't stop safely? Do you swerve into oncoming traffic on your left or into a tree on your right, or do you hit the animal?"

I realized there was nothing I could have done to avoid the chipmunk, but clearly, there's some bad blood between me and the rodent population. My photo must be on a "Wanted" sign somewhere deep in the underbrush of the chipmunk lodge.

I'll tell you what—that Conkle's Hollow chipmunk got off easy.

The Olingo disappears into the forest blackness.

I see my murderous reputation has reached Costa Rica.
Continuing along the trail, Diego leads us into the center of an alcove, a courtyard kind of area totally surrounded by extremely tall trees.

"Shine your flashlights into the tree tops," Diego instructs.

All fifteen or so lights point up to see hundreds of bright green things clumped and curled amongst the branches, about 30 feet overhead, swaying and dangling in the breeze like spiral wind spinners you get at the dollar store.

"These are highly poisonous snakes," states Diego as if it's supposed to make us feel more at ease.

Snakes.

Remembering the snake encounter in La Fortuna, I should be hyperventilating and frozen in place, but something else is happening inside of me this time.

I'm *not* terrified that one of these green reptiles could drop out of the trees and land on my head at any moment. Is it because they're so high above me that I'm not reacting with fear? I know

I'm trapped by the crowd behind me and can't escape, but I'm not feeling claustrophobic either.

What I do feel, is swelling laughter. I begin a high-pitched, maniacal laugh.

"Chihuly!" I squeal out loud when I finally catch my breath and throw my hands up in the air. "I'm in a hanging snake garden," laughing so hard my side begins to hurt.

These lime-green spirals and curly-que things don't look like snakes hanging so far above my head. They look like blown-glass sculptures by Dale Chihuly, an American contemporary glass artist whose work is defined by "asymmetry and irregularity."

Some years ago, I saw a stunning glass sculpture created by Chihuly called "Sol del Citron" at Fairchild Tropical Botanic Gardens in Coral Gables, Florida. With the exception of a slight color enhancement towards the lime side, what I'm looking at could easily be his blown glass sculptures, twisting and curling among the branches of the trees. The "artwork" similarities strike me as hilarious.

"Look, it's the work of Chihuly," I say still laughing as I turn to share my perspective on the spiraled snakes.

I am the only one left in the circle.

Perhaps the sight of a crazed cackling woman below venomous snakes that could drop at any moment was more than they could stomach.

Perhaps there's a reason they left. Perhaps I should go, too.

I catch up with the group outside of the snake garden and try to share my vision of blown glass sculptures, but everyone keeps a good distance from me.

We exit the forest walking towards the parking lot, the guides point their flashlights into the trees again showing us Three-Toed Sloths. They're so high in the tree tops, they look more like large gray nests Big Bird might roost in on Sesame Street. Nothing about these big gray blobs resembles an animal to my eyes. Maybe if I get a closer look...

Dammit! I forgot to bring the freakin' binoculars. Oh, well, I did have that close encounter with the sloth in the parking lot back at *Ecocentro Danaus.* That will have to do.

We pile back into the vans for our hotels.

Funny, no one challenges me for the front seat.

ZIPPING INTO MY SIXTIES

Today is my birthday.

I assemble the items I'll need for today's adventures, and I can't stop smiling. I'm happy. Happier than I've been on most of my birthdays.

Until now, my favorite birthday had been "South Pacific." It was the first birthday following the divorce. For months beforehand, my best friend Carla would take my children while I went to counseling, but little did I know what she had them doing.

My birthday arrived and another of my friends, Pat, took me out to lunch and shopping. Upon returning home, I opened the front door to my house to find smoke.

"What the hell? Call 9-1-1!" I screamed. As the smoke cleared, I could make out monstrous palm fronds leaning up against my walls and sliding glass doors.

"Surprise!"

The lights came on and I turned to find the women from my homeschooling group dressed in tropical prints with leis around their necks. They'd transformed my entire living room into the stage setting for the musical "South Pacific."

The show began complete with music, costumes, and a fog machine with our collective children as the stars. They'd memorized the script and the words to the songs, even the dance steps. This explained why my kids went around for weeks singing songs from a musical they'd never seen.

That was the best birthday anyone had ever thrown for me.

Zip lining in Costa Rica is the best birthday I could ever give myself.

I Googled what to wear when zip lining in Monteverde, so

I strut my stuff past the mirror looking like a model for an American outdoorsman magazine.

And next on our fashion runway is Teresa geared up in her black Ahnu hiking boots and gray Smartwool socks ready to challenge the zip line. She's coordinated these with a pair of charcoal stretch capris ensuring freedom of movement. Continuing this free moving theme, she's wearing a matching layered look of day-glow orange sports bra, tank top, and long-sleeve quick-dry pullover with half-zippered neckline adding just a bit more zip to the zip line. Topping off her fashionable ensemble is a men's Northface rain jacket in forest green, and khaki Tilley adventure hat.

The online tips had suggested wearing stuff that could be thrown away after zip lining because grease and dirt from the line get all over your clothing and can be difficult to remove, especially without laundry facilities. Ticos frown on tourists beating their clothes with a rock in their sparkling clean streams.

I exit my hotel room, my cheeks ache from the colossal grin on my face as there's a beautiful rainbow arched above my hotel formed by the rainforest mist. A promise that I will not die on the zip-line today.

The bus picks me up, along with some other "zippers," and we're off. Enthusiasm radiates through my freshly blow-dried hair and makeup. We arrive at the zip line building whose lobby is filled with equipment and a big screen TV playing a promo video of zippers giving their opinions on the activity.

"Next," shouts the cashier.

"Hola! I've already paid," I show them my voucher.

"Go through that back door and someone will show you what to do next."

134

I follow his pointing arm and once outside, I am met by another guy with a camera.

"Stand over there and let me take your picture," said the photographer.

"Is this in case you need a photo to identify my body should I fall to a horrible death, assuming there's anything left of it?"

He laughs and snaps a couple of pictures then shows me to the lockers on the side of the main building where I store my purple CamelBak hydration pack, Tilley adventure hat, and camera. He said you can't have anything in your hands, but I think storing stuff in a locker makes it easier for them to collect your personal affects when you die.

We get fitted with safety harnesses, train-sized coupling hooks, bright red crash dummy helmets — so much for my beautifully coiffed hair — and lumberjack leather gloves. I'm stunning.

The guides lead us out through the foliage to bleachers where we all sit like the crowd ready to cheer on a football team. We receive a crash course — maybe a poor choice of words — in how to negotiate the line, where to put our hands and how to carry our bodies.

The instructor continues, "It's very, very important that you keep your ankles crossed and stay in a seated position. Your leather-palm gloves grab hold of the line and the firmness of your grip controls your speed." They didn't say, however, what would happen if you didn't stay in that seated position.

"Any questions?" the instructor asked.

"Yes," I raised my gloved hand. "What happens if you don't stay in the seated position with your ankles crossed?"

Without missing a beat, the instructor said matter-of-factly, "We divide up your personal belongings."

"Okay, grab your hooks and follow us." The guides lead us

off to the left and up a metal scaffold.

I watch as one by one they clip onto the line with their heavy metal hook and sail off into the mist. It's strange. I don't have butterflies or nervous anxiety, but I'm excited. I feel confident and thrilled to be doing this on my sixtieth birthday. I feel young and my world is vibrant.

As we wait in line, I sound like a six-year-old child as I repeat to anyone within earshot, "Today's my birthday," but I resist the almost overwhelming urge to hold up fingers to show my age.

It's my turn. It's here, the moment that drove me to come to Costa Rica. The activity that would define my sixtieth birthday. I review in my head the instructions the guides gave us during our pre-zip crash course. The guide takes the huge hook from my hands and clips it onto the zip line. "Remember to keep your ankles crossed. You decide how fast to go with how hard you grip the line," he reminds me.

In about thirty feet, the zip line ahead of me disappears into the clouds. The guide sends me off with one more reminder about keeping my ankles crossed.

My feet leave the platform and I slip off into the cloud. What had been a soft mist against my skin quickly turns into a thousand little needles stinging my face, but the thrill of gliding through the air outweighs the slight annoyance of such a puny pain. Moving through a scratchy wool blanket of clouds around me with the stunning green below me, and feeling no fear is extraordinary. I wonder if this is what it feels like to hang glide. I don't feel like a bird flying. I feel more like…like I'm floating. I'm free from all earthly constraints, and barely notice the line whizzing through my hand or what my ass must look like in this harness.

My feet touch down on the platform at the other side.

"How was it?" the guide on the other side asks as he unhooks me from the line.

"INCREDIBLE!" I shout at the top of my lungs.

"Do you want to do it again?"

"I sure do!" Maybe I'll come back tomorrow."

"Tomorrow? You have twelve more to go today."

I look up the side of the mountain. A steep climb regardless of what shape you're in. Is he serious?

"Huh? I thought it was a one and done thing! I must have missed that piece of information in the brochure," I stammered, trying to not sound whinny. Apparently, the course is made up of thirteen lines, each separated by a hike mostly straight up a mountainside.

Now the fear shows up. I look from the mountain to the guide and back again. I don't know if I can do this.

Okay. I have to go. Hiking boots don't fail me now.

I stop a few yards up the hill and again in another few feet, far too often in order to catch my breath, and at one juncture, the tallest guide hooks his arm under mine and literally drags me up the mountain.

Gasping for air, I begin to wonder if I'm really an emphysema patient.

"Monteverde," says the guide still dragging me, "straddles the Continental Divide at 4,921 feet. That's 1,500 meters of elevation. Do you have emphysema?"

Jackass.

There are multiple groups of about five to seven people and six guides per group, late twenty-something men all in excellent condition. Then there's me. Even the couple in their late '70s with their tall, lithe figures pass me on the trail. She's wearing tight teal exercise capris, a long sleeve magenta shirt, a navy down vest, and teal hiking shoes. Color coordinated. Bitch. He's in tight

137

charcoal leggings, a grey and red plaid shirt, black down vest, and black hiking shoes. Looking as though they went to the same outdoor fashion show as I did. They're not even breaking a sweat or breathing hard. I hate them.

We come to one very long and significantly higher gorge.

One guide hooks me up to the line and says, "He's going to go with you," motioning to another guide. Guide #2 hooks onto the line in front of me, and Guide #1 says, "Now, wrap your legs around him."

"W-w-what?"

"Go on. Wrap your legs around him," Guide #1 repeats.

I'm not attracted to them, although they're fit and cute. Hell, with the helmets and olive green jumpers, I can barely tell them apart, but I'll make the most of the situation. I oblige my instructors, but not without making a lot of suggestive moans and comments while doing it.

Off we soar into the cloud with me shouting, "Ooo-la-la!" "Oh, baby!" "Yes, yes, yes!" "Faster! Faster!" and other provocative sounds. We reach the other side and snickers and laughter await me at the platform.

I purred to Guide #2, "Was it good for you?"

We fly on though the course. Well, they all fly but drag me up the steep incline like a bag full of potatoes, cracking jokes in Spanish, probably at my expense.

Defeat set in and I kicked myself for not reading the pamphlet more closely. What was I thinking? I'm out of breath and my lungs feel like they're about to burst.

"Enough," I exhale breathlessly. "I can't do it. Leave me here."

"We can't leave you here! How do you plan to stay alive out here alone? You can do it. Besides, we help you." Ignoring my pleas for abandonment, they hoist me up by the elbows and pull me up the mountain.

Just when I think I can't take another step, we came to another very high and lengthy line. The other tourists have already zipped down the line ahead of me.

Guide #1 says, "He's going to go with you again."

I hear a voice in my right ear from Guide #2. "Do you want me in back this time?"

"Oh, yes," I said in a sultry voice, but mostly because I'm out of breath.

"Be gentle with me," I croak. "I'm new to this. Take it slow."

"I'll go as slow as you want me to, baby" he responds.

The sexual banter continues as he hooks onto the zip line behind my head and wraps his legs around me. Off we go, both of us screaming wild erotic sounds that would make monkeys blush. We arrive at the platform on the other end, to the sight of guides and tourists alike bent over in hysterics. I give my zip line mate a giant hug and thank him for an awesome time.

He murmurs, "So, it was good for you, yes?"

"The best I've ever had," my smile nearly splitting my face.

With renewed vigor from the ride, we climb upward again toward the next line. The ground becomes slippery under my boots from the mist. A couple of people without proper shoes slide back down and end up crawling on their hands and knees to make it to the platform. I would pat myself on the back for having made such a wise decision in buying these hiking boots if I wasn't busy gasping for air like a white-water rafting guide caught under a Goliath Grouper.

On the next line, I stop short of the platform by about twenty to thirty feet and have to be rescued.

"Now what," I yell ahead to the guide on the platform. For the first time, I felt the emptiness under me, and I clamped my gloved hand tighter around the zip line.

"Sit still. I come get you."

To get rescued means that one of the guides from the receiving platform hooks onto the line, throws his legs up and wraps his ankles around the line, and pulls himself out to me the stranded party. Once out there, he wraps his legs around my legs then pulls us both, hand over hand, forward to the platform. Picture dragonflies mating on a clothesline.

By the time my savior pulls us back onto the platform, he is drenched in sweat. My Spanish dictionary was back in the locker, but I'm sure I'm hearing multiple curse words, and I think he's making disparaging remarks about sexually inactive well-fed female cattle.

Several tourists in my group are also stopping short of the platform making me feel more assured, including the older couple that chose to go "Superman" style. That's where you lay flat out in the air hooked onto the line from the center of your back, staring straight down into the crevasse.

I watched as the seventy-year old woman flying Superman style stops out in the middle, staring at the tops of the trees in the gully beneath her. She just hung there. I couldn't tell if she was just waiting for assistance or if she was too terrified to move, but she didn't scream. I guess that's the difference ten years in age can make in your composure. Staring into the abyss doesn't scare you at seventy because you stare it down on a daily basis.

Maybe on a return trip, I'll go Superman style, but for this journey, I'm content zipping my way through the forest following the airlines' recommended advice of "seat backs in their full and upright positions."

EPIPHANY

Adrenaline rushes through my cholesterol-soaked veins after zip lining. I reluctantly turn in my line gear and deposit a twenty-dollar bill into the tip jar.

A much better use of a twenty than the dinner I had with the homeless man.

I collect my belongings from the locker, and welcome the hike along the *Hanging Bridges* adjacent to the zip-lining center as a way of winding down.

The beginning of the trail is only *slightly* inclined, so I shouldn't need an arm from a guide to drag me uphill.

Moisture collects on my face.

"Is that rain?" I ask the employee at the entrance to the bridges.

"No, not rain. Clouds moving through the trees make the lightweight mist. We call it 'cat hair'."

It doesn't make my clothes wet like rain would, just an accumulated bead of water now and then.

"It gives nutrients to the epiphytes that live in the trees with no roots to the soil," he explains.

Maybe this cat hair will rejuvenate my skin to the point that I'll leave the forest looking nine years younger or at least have nine more lives. Regardless, it feels invigorating, much softer than the needle pokes it gave me on the zip line.

The cat hair collects on the trees creating swollen droplets that gently roll off the leaves and plop softly onto the foliage below creating a rhythmic oratorio with each movement being a new cantata. Those rain sticks got this sound right. Maybe I'll buy one when I get back to remind me of this sound. I'll have to keep flipping it over, though.

I didn't opt for the guided tour of the *Hanging Bridges*, and

I'm so happy with my choice. Being alone gives me the freedom to move along at my own pace and stop from time to time just to drink in the solitude of this place. I am at peace here.

Trudging through forests is in my blood. As a child living in the countryside of Ohio, my brother and I, along with our trusty Bassett Hound, Scamp, would traverse muddy rivulets and scale miniature mountains in the woods behind our house. When most perceived a large stone, we saw a boulder climb in Yosemite National Park. Scrawny trickles of a creek held the mysteries of the deepest seas, the opportunity to study the effects of dam building, and to investigate the monsters of the deep that lived under rocks.

When I was in the second grade and we moved into the city, I feared our nature explorations might be over until my brother discovered the back road to Adena, the 2,000-acre home of Ohio's sixth governor, Thomas Worthington. It was the view looking east from the north lawn of Adena that inspired the Great Seal of Ohio, and a perfect place for reconnoitering, albeit illegal. Boatloads of kids from the neighborhood could be found tromping through the stream that ran alongside the access road, swinging through the trees from grapevines, or scurrying across the grounds willy-nilly, experiencing the freedom that only a large open space can bring to a child.

I enjoyed the stream in all seasons; watching the changing colors of the leaves float by in fall, walking on the ice in winter while the water flowed beneath it, and petting the fluffy moss and lichens in spring that grew along its margin.

In Costa Rica amidst the clouds of Monteverde, large clumps of moss have formed on the trunks of the towering trees in alternating patterns like grips on a rock-climbing wall, nothing like the ground moss and lichens we found along the creek beds in Ohio. Because of the climate and highly specialized

144

ecosystems, cloud forests are host to endemic species and are a habitat like no other anywhere else on Earth.

In addition to the clumps of moss, there is an epiphyte that grows in long rope-like tendrils from the tops of the trees down towards the forest floor.

I wonder if I could use these to swing from tree to tree like Tarzan.

Ah, yeah...Jon Tarzan, me Jane. He'd look hot dressed like the Ape Man or undressed like him, I guess I should say.

The temptation to run my fingertips over the velvety surface of the moss or test my swinging theory on the tendrils is almost too much, but I resist, stuffing my hands in my pockets.

Although not nearly as strenuous, the trail is similar to the zip line in that you walk a portion then you cross a bridge, then you repeat. For the first chunk of the trail, the clouds hang low around me in a soothing fog. But once the clouds part, the view from the Hanging Bridges is spectacular. I snap a photo of a stunning tree that looks like it might be from a Tarzan movie with its massive spreading branches. A strangler fig, perhaps. I'm up so high on the bridge that I'm staring down at it like it's a shrub on the ground below my fifth floor apartment back home.

It's nice to be in the presence of something older than myself besides the seventy-year old couple who kicked my butt climbing the mountainside.

I encounter four large millipedes, Python Millipedes according to my nature guide, racing along the pathway. One wasn't fast enough. With all those legs, you'd think it could out-run stupid humans hurrying by with no other goal than to get to the end of the path. Why even bother coming here if you're going to hastily brush past all the rainforest has to offer?

I want to yell at them, "You're missing it!"

I saunter along the path stepping off to the side when the

speed-walkers scurry past. Something the millipede was probably trying to do, too.

I stand in this earthly cathedral beneath clustered columns of trees with sharply pointed spires stretching toward heaven. The sound of the forest symphony swells to a crescendo in my ears. Sunlight filters down through the leaves like light passing through a yellow stained glass window, splitting into thousands of golden orbs, scattered throughout the atmosphere and washing over my body. I close my eyes as I adore this euphoric moment.

"You don't need a man to be all right. You are enough."

What? Did I hear you correctly?

I don't whip around to see who is talking. I know this voice. I've heard it many times in my life, but these words? Always before, the messages had to do with others, nothing to do with my merit.

I can pick such times off the top of my head when I've heard God so concisely; the time I had the courage to stay with my husband; the time I was told I would have a baby; the time my son almost got hit by a car; and the time I saved a stranger's life in the hospital.

As newlyweds in 1978, my now ex-husband and I took a vacation with both sets of our parents. Not the best of ideas. We were in the Smokey Mountains about to part company with my parents heading off to the North and his parents heading to the South with us. The parents crossed the highway to a restaurant leaving my husband and me to hash out our differences over something ridiculous. True to his routine, he told me if I didn't like his approach it was either his way or the highway. Well, there was the highway and there was my father's truck. So, I tossed my things into the bed of the truck and said Sayōnara to my husband.

My husband crossed the highway to the restaurant with

146

the other family members leaving me alone in the empty parking lot to contemplate my choice.

"You belong with him," a voice said.

I looked around to see who was saying such a repugnant statement, but there was no one. I realized who was speaking, though, much to my chagrin, after a brief argument with God, I complied with the request and pulled my things from my dad's truck and headed south towards Miami with my husband.

The next time I remember hearing His voice so loud and succinct, it took me by surprise again.

There would be no third child in our lives. I had some physical issues and my husband decided we were done with the baby-making production. However, I have learned to never assume where God is concerned.

While shopping for a baby gift for my cousin in a now defunct department store called Burdines, I heard a voice speak to me.

"You will have a son and you will name him Aaron Andrew."

"I'm sorry. What did you say?" I asked the two women shopping next to me.

"We didn't say anything to you. We weren't even speaking," they said as they distanced themselves from me.

Ah, I thought. *You're imagining things. Probably just wishful thinking, perhaps. Certainly not God.*

I never said a word to anyone about the message, let alone my husband. It had to be my own thoughts. We weren't having another child.

Two years later, I lay on a delivery room table after giving birth to my third child, a son. My husband went off to the hospital nursery to see how much the baby weighed. After a short time, he came dashing back into the delivery room, shoulders bowed

147

forward, his hands clasped to his chest, and tears running out of his eyes.

"Oh, my, God, what's wrong? Is there something wrong with the baby!" I said in a panic, trying to get up off the table.

"No, no, he's fine," he said reassuring me. He paused for a long time before continuing and said, "God just spoke to me and said I was to name him Aaron Andrew."

Three years later, the same son, the girls, and I, exit the grocery store when the voice says, "Grab him. He's going to run."

I latched onto my son's arm, but he wrenched out of my grip and darted between parked cars into the path of an oncoming vehicle. It happened too fast. I couldn't reach him in time. I saw my son slam hard into something and bounce back, splayed out onto the pavement.

I screamed. I breathed in little sips of air as if to make time stop in its tracks.

"I didn't see him. He just appeared out of nowhere," the driver howled an ashen face. "Thank God you got to him in time. Which one of you stopped him?"

"We didn't," we answered in disbelief.

My son sat up unscathed. He had not been hit by the car. Looking under my son's clothing, there wasn't a bruise on him, not even a red mark from an impact. He had run into something unseen a split second before the car screeched to a stop.

"Are you hurt?" I asked, continuing to inspect him from head to toe. "What did you run into?"

"The man," was all my son could tell us.

I heard the voice again years later in the throes of divorce, and I became hospitalized toward the end of mediations. I sat in the hospital lunchroom staring down at my plate across from a man eating his slices of roast beef, when I heard the voice say,

"Watch. Be ready. He's going to choke."

I looked up and watched as the man began to choke. No attendants or nurses could be seen in the room to help this guy and no one around him noticed what was happening. I had to help him. I looked around the room and saw a phone. I leapt up from the table and called for help as the man turned blue and dropped to the floor.

"We need help in the cafeteria. A man is choking," I anxiously shouted into the phone.

I ran back to the man now purple, lying motionless. I could see the whites of his eyes and he was no longer grasping his throat. People sitting around the room just went right on eating lunch like nothing was happening. Three attendants and several attempts of the Heimlich maneuver finally cleared the man's airway and got him breathing.

"Thank you for your quick response," the nurses said patting me on the back. "He would have died if you hadn't done something."

I really couldn't take the credit.

But now the voice is saying something new — about me.
How can I be "enough?"

I had tried to be perfect. I stayed married to a man I loved like the voice told me to do. I wore the right clothes. Lived in the right neighborhood. Behaved the right way, and attended church regularly.

But instead of these choices making me feel approved, they left me feeling empty and insecure. I always felt as if I had fallen short of perfection, like I had to make all the right choices without error or I wouldn't get my gold star of acceptance.

Then one day, it hit me — his hand. This wasn't the first physical encounter with my ex-husband, but this time it was in front my daughter. I felt like Snow White awakening from her

149

long sleep, suddenly being present in a world where time had marched on in her absence. Where had I been the past eighteen years? Walking on eggshells and trying not to blemish the perfect picture of our lives left me not knowing who I was. In the eight years prior to having children and the six years of being a stay-at-home mom, I hadn't so much as written a check, let alone paid a bill. I was completely and totally dependent upon him for everything.

This awakening was not to a happier-ever-after life, but to a nightmare of self-doubt. My feelings of unworthiness just got worse, and the voices in my head convinced me that I was never going to be enough. I'm sure God was trying to get my attention, but my neediness was so loud it obscured His voice.

God may have always known I was enough, but I couldn't buy into it. My marriage as well as numerous subsequent other relationships failed. I had no college degrees to fall back on. No money in the bank. I sold my house and quit going to church after one pastor was found to be having an affair with one of the parishioners and another skipped the country after being found guilty of child molestation. He was the youth minister. I lost faith in the church. The forging of my dirty deeds chain grew in production and became as long as the chain Jacob Marley forged in his lifetime in Dicken's "Christmas Carol."

But here, now, in the serenity of nature's cathedral, I hear Him.

You don't need a man to be all right.

I no longer need to suffer that empty longing for a man to complete me or take care of me. Fears of abandonment no longer leave me desperate and clingy for any man who looks twice in my direction. I am free to choose companionship or solo travel, relationship or solitude.

I realize I have been using the wrong ruler to see if I

measured up.

My heart is overwhelmed with gratitude knowing that I am acceptable just as I am, and I begin to weep tears of joy. My soul is lifted up into the atmosphere along with the sun-filtered orbs, and my feet don't touch the ground. My arms rise toward heaven, embracing His presence and thanking Him for His many blessings.

However, punctuality isn't one of them.

I'm alone in the rainforest experiencing one of the most deeply spiritual moments of my life and realize the speed walkers are no longer zooming past me. I suspect that I have missed my bus back to the hotel. Maybe that's the reason they were hurrying along the path.

Don't worry. Be happy. Ooh, ooh ooh ooh oo-ooh...

I finish the trail at a leisurely pace enjoying everything nature is showing me. Eventually, I arrive back at the welcome center as the sun hangs low behind the trees.

"We were just about to send people out to find you," said a young member of the staff. "Are you alright?"

"Yes, thank you. Couldn't be better, actually. I appreciate your concern, and I'm sorry I made you worry."

"We held the last bus for you."

"Thank you, sugar." I climb onto the waiting bus.

"Hello, everyone." I greeted a different group of adventurers from this morning.

"Hola!" "Hello," the greetings come back.

I recognize a couple of speed racers, but choose not to mention the carnage they left behind on the trail.

"Aren't you the one whose birthday is today?" someone asked.

"Yes, I am," I answered again becoming that six year old

child.

"What an awesome thing to do on your birthday!" one remarked.

"How did you come to choose Costa Rica?" another asked.

I tell them the story of my boss's daughter, "and besides, it's inexpensive, close by, and I get a stamp on my virgin passport. What more could I ask for?"

"Who came with you?" someone asked.

"No one. I brought myself." Then add, "I'm enough."

These guys are pleasant, talkative, and fun. What a difference from the morning bus ride.

Or maybe what's different is me. Instead of crawling along life's trail like the millipedes, perhaps the view of myself has been elevated to where I can see people as fellow journeymen and not as speed walkers poised to crush me underfoot.

The bus driver stops alongside the highway, and points out large gray blobs in the tops of the trees about a football field away. "Sloths," he says.

Can't prove it by me. Just grey nests from here.

Perhaps if I could get my binoculars out of my backpack, I might be able to see them, but he pulls back onto the road and drives away while I'm still searching. Cheated once again out of another sloth sighting. Maybe I don't need a man, but I need more sloths.

The bus drops me off at my hotel, and I walk down the hill to my room. I sit on my back patio, looking out across the hills, the mist flows down off the mountaintop and into the ravine below me like one of those misting fans at Disney on a hot Florida day. The strong wind creates a rolling howl through the lower elevations that moves back up the side of the mountains, and races through the treetops next to me. The howl swells to a crescendo then trails off into the hills. The clouds, what few there are, gallop by in a race to the sea.

152

Millipedes

PIZZA AND BEER

My aching muscles strain to climb up the steep hill from my room to the hotel lobby. I haven't eaten since early morning, and another protein bar just ain't gonna cut it. I'm taking myself out for a birthday dinner, cupcake in hand.

Where are my strong zip lining guides when I need them?

Dragging myself up the hill, I reach the door to the hotel feeling every bit my age. A group of fellow zippers are standing by the front desk.

"Hey, isn't today your birthday?" one of them asks. "How are you going to celebrate?"

"I picked up this cupcake yesterday from a bakery by the coffee shop," I say, holding up the bakery bag while trying to catch my breath.

"Oh, that's pathetic," they scoff, "we insist you join us for dinner. We're getting pizza at the place down the street."

"I'd love to."

With cupcake in hand, I walk with them to the Italian restaurant a short distance from the hotel. There, other adventurers are already seated around tables that have been pulled together in preparation for a larger group.

"Hey, it's the birthday girl!" a man shouts.

"I brought my birthday cake to share with you all." I hold up the miniscule bag.

"I brought my bottle of wine to share," another announced, holding a bottle of Santa Rita Secret Reserve Red Blend wine from Chile. We all pour a "shot" from the bottle into our glasses and drink a toast to the day.

I could slug down that whole bottle right now.

Three pizzas with various toppings are shared around the table. The Costa Rica pizza masquerading as Italian food is outstanding, but then, I've never met a pizza I didn't like. I pick up the knife and cut the cupcake into little cubes to share.

I should just pass the knife around and let the people lick it since that's about all they're going to get.

Everyone pulls out cameras and cell phones to share pictures and stories of their experiences from the day.

"Did you see the howler monkeys in that tree?" one woman asks pointing to the giant Tarzan tree I had photographed from the hanging bridge.

No, but I saw one floating down a river in board shorts, I thought with a sneer.

"You saw monkeys?" I ask.

"Yes, they were sitting in that very tree as we went past it," she said, "I think we went through there before you, though."

"Damn it! I've seen almost every critter on my list except for those freakin' monkeys," I'm green inside. Chartreuse through and through for sure. "Can you send me your picture of the monkeys so I can tell everyone I took it?"

They laugh.

"Were you the one shouting all those X-rated things on the zip line?" the blonde to my left asks.

"Did it sound something like this: 'Ooo, baby! Oo-la-la! Faster, faster!' Any of those sound familiar?" I answered with a mischievous grin.

"It was you? That was hysterical," they howled.

Food and conversations all shared around the table make for a fabulous evening with total strangers. I've cracked open the door in the wall I've built around myself trusting that I won't be rejected, and my world hasn't caved in. I think back to the tree in La Fortuna filled with various colorful birds. This time I get to be the Cherries Tanager sitting amongst a smorgasbord of friendly fliers.

156

We leave in separate directions with the feeling as though I've known them for years. I am so grateful they included me in their evening, but more thankful that I risked shedding my shell of insecurity.

I'm not ready to call it a night, so I stop at the bar for a drink.

"What would you like?" asks the waitress as I sit down at a table.

"What beer do you have?"

She lists off a few names, most of which I don't recognize.

"Can you bring me one that's made here in Costa Rica?" I ask.

"Si," and off she goes to retrieve the beer. She returns with a bottle named "Imperial Silver" in English across the front and a frosty mug. The waitress pops the top and pours the amber liquid into the mug. I take a gulp.

Oh my God, that's disgusting! Bitter, disappointing swill.

I force a smile at the waitress and give her a thumbs-up sign. She walks away.

Then two dogs walk into a bar.

Sounds like the beginning of an old joke.

A Dachshund with another larger, hairier stray swagger in through the open door of the bar like they own the place.

"Umm, excuse me, bartender, but some dogs just walked in," I say certain it would be a health violation.

"Ah, not to worry. They're regulars here," he says.

The dogs move with an intentional slowness visiting first one table then the next looking for handouts. They saunter over to the right side of my chair and sit down looking at me expectedly.

"Sorry guys, but all I can offer you is this crappy beer," I tell them. They continue to stare at me, so I put my hand down

157

to pet them. Slowly they rise up off their haunches, sniff my hand, realize there's nothing in it, and stride away with a put-off kind of attitude.

Ingrates.

Then it occurs to me that I am the strange stray in this neighborhood and obviously not aware that there's a tariff to pay to these guys when in their establishment. Normally, sitting unaccompanied in a bar at night would be cause for me to feel alienated and unwanted, but I feel quite content as I confidently stray into unknown territory like I own the place.

The beer is, meh, so I do the equivalent of holding my nose and chug it down like bad cough syrup. I ask the waitress to bring me something made with Cacique, my new favorite liquor. I suck down the first of two drinks, reflecting upon the glorious birthday I am having. For the first time since this morning, I've slowed down and thought about Jon. I would like to see him, but I realized his presence or any other man's presence today is unnecessary. I'm having a great time with whomever comes my way.

Whoa. You're starting to wax philosophical. No more drinks for you. Time to call it a night.

I leave the bar and make it down the steep hill to my room in spite of the alcohol, brush my teeth, and fall into bed. The air smells so delicious that I get back up and open my sliding glass doors to the outside, leaving just the screen doors to separate me from the rainforest. Risky, since anyone walking around the building could simply walk right in like the dogs in the bar, but there's nothing more relaxing than sleeping with the windows open on a cool windy evening. It's something I don't often get to experience back in Florida. Just to be cautious, though, I slip my knife under my pillow.

As I settle back into bed, the breeze blows in through the

open sliders and lightly wafts over my bare skin, perking up the peach fuzz along my shoulders. I shimmy down under the blanket a bit further, and roll onto my side thinking of Jon, and how nice it would have been to share the events of my birthday with him. I am enough, but I like the idea of his companionship.

My breathing becomes slower and heavier as I drift off to dream.

A warm hand slides around my waist from behind me and under my arm to gently pull me closer. I hear his breathing next to my ear. His smell is intoxicating, like the freshness of the mountain air blowing through the window resonating the exotic fragrance of the Queen of the Night flowers. My body relaxes against his.

"You're here. I've been waiting for you," I whisper. He caresses my waist and brushes his fingers lightly over my skin making it contract into goose bumps. His nose nuzzles my ear as he gently kisses along my neck. I can feel his body hard against mine, pressing against my back, and I know this night will be one of ecstasy.

He rolls me onto my back and kisses me fully on the mouth. I moan for more. I run my right hand along his side and across his back, feeling each muscle flex and release as he moves his chest onto mine. The sensation of skin against skin is electric as one passion absorbs into the other. My fingers entwine themselves in his thick black hair, and I try not to pull, too hard. I relish in his touch knowing what is to come. He whispers something in Spanish that sets me tingling all over as my breathing increases with anticipation. I feel the warmth of his tongue sliding across my breast, as sighs of heady desire escape my throat. I haven't experienced this much pleasure in forever. I wrap my leg over his hips, and my body turns to liquid as I give myself completely over to his influence.

B & B VISTA ATENAS

I don't want to leave.

Can I find a job in this area without speaking Spanish, and what of housing? Where would I live? Can I live indefinitely in a hostel? And what of my family back in the U.S.? Will anyone miss me if I stay? I sigh deeply knowing the answers and hand my luggage over to the shuttle driver. I'm leaving Monteverde by way of bus up and over the mountains as opposed to taking the boat ride across Lake Arenal, like on my arrival.

The green vistas stretch up the mountainside out my shuttle window rolling like waves, only instead of crashing onto a sandy shore, these waves roll off into the horizon of azure skies. I can't contain a grin. It breaks across my face and takes away a bit of the bitterness of departure. My lungs take in the fresh mountain air reminding me of Jon and last night's dream. His presence in my bed was the most tangible experience I've ever had in a dream.

Call him. Why should I? He's made no attempt to contact me.

My phone has no bars up here amongst the clouds.

You've had no signal. He couldn't reach you. I don't need a man, remember. Yeah, but what if you want one?

We travel south out of the rainforest towards my last hotel stay, and a pang of regret lies heavy in my stomach.

You're not dead, you know. Last night's dream proved that.

This time in Costa Rica has brought me the joy and exuberance of youth I had lost along the way when practicing to be an adult. Every cell in my body seems to have come alive with the tingling desire to experience existence once more. Instead of looking down the line towards my eventual death, I'm looking towards the discoveries waiting on the other side of the fog.

We pull into the B & B Vista Atenas Hotel, a one-story

building perched on the side of a steep mountain. It looks like an Art Deco motel from old Florida Keys with a little South American flavor dusted over it. The L-shaped building is painted sand beige with mango-colored trim. Off to the left is a two-story building with the same color combination where the Belgian owner, Vera Fouriau, lives.

Fouriau visited Cost Rica several years ago and fell in love with the country the moment she stepped off the plane, not unlike my experience. She and her husband dreamed of starting up a bed 'n breakfast, and when Fouriau discovered Vista Atenas, she knew this was her place. The rooms are pleasant and clean, but the real attraction at Hotel Vista Atenas is the pool area with a stunning view of the Central Valley below.

The plan upon arrival at the B & B Vista Atenas Hotel is to have a couple of days lounging by the pool, relaxing with a tropical drink, and taking in the pristine view from the chaise lounge following my busy week.

That lasted for about fifteen minutes.

Lounging around just isn't enough. I can't stand the idea of wasting a minute of this beautiful country. So I speak with Vera over a cup of delicious coffee.

"Vera, the flavor of this coffee is outstanding."

"Thank you," she answers. "I purchase it from a local grower."

"Your bed and breakfast is lovely, but I just feel like I'm missing out on something by sitting around. Is there some place I can go or something to see nearby?"

Her face lit up like a Christmas tree.

"The coffee farm nearby does tours," she said. "Would you like me to see if they will give you a tour tomorrow?"

"Absolutely," I exclaimed. "But, I need to buy a couple of things today. Is there a grocery store nearby?"

Silly question. Everything's nearby when you have taxis. Moments later, a little red taxi slides into the driveway, and off I go to the grocery.

The taxi drops me off at the "Supermercado Coopeatenas" and speeds away. It's a busy place. I walk in and heads turn.

Girl, you must look good.

I would like to think it is my stunningly fashionable outfit of purple short-sleeved, sweat-wicking V-neck shirt, khaki capris, adventure hat, black hiking boots and royal blue backpack. But, likely the attention I've garnered is more like a, "I know everyone in this town, and she doesn't belong here" look.

My shopping list is short: toothpaste, fruit, bottles of *Lizano* to smuggle back to Florida, and cheese. However, the excitement of recognizing things with names in Spanish is too much fun, and I linger in every aisle, trying to pronounce each new word. I find the bakery, of course, and pick up a few unknown pastries. More monkey brains, I presume, but delicious, nonetheless. I pick through the clothing, hats, and other trinkets before facing the line of cashiers. I move from checkout to checkout cocking my head to one side listening for a cashier who might speak English. I feel like Jon facing the choice at the airport trying to pick out the right customs agent. *I wonder why he did that.* I take the plunge and pick one, a young woman with a friendly face.

"Hola!" I say with a smile as wide as Texas, figuring that if I look friendly, she won't rip me off when it comes time to pay. My math sucks in America, but in Costa Rica, it's an industrial vacuum cleaner.

"Hello," she replied. "You here from America?"

"Yes. What gave me away?" I asked. "The touristy clothes or the clueless look on my face?"

She laughs and asks, "Do you want the total in American

dollars or in colones?"

Now, it was my turn to laugh. I think I know what a second grade kid must feel like when trying to count out change at a candy store for the first time and relieved when an adult steps in.

"Let's stick with something I know. American dollars, please," I say breathing a sigh of relief.

I leave the grocery store and decide to investigate the "downtown" area of Atenas. The weather is lovely so I choose to walk. Not really certain where I'm headed, I just keep to what I think is the main road. That works until the road splits and the left side of it heads off into the hills and I'm forced to make a choice. I stay to the right toward a residential area of single-family residences that don't appear to have just single families living in them. Each porch or yard is bristling with activity with adults and children. I wonder how many people they can cram into these tiny houses.

On my right, sitting smack dab in the middle of the houses, I come up to what appears to be a karate dojo with no walls. Just a roof, poles, and a concrete floor, sort of a very large tiki hut. There are children of all ages standing straight and tall as they practice their kata choreography. Only a couple of the older students wear a gi with tied belts. I stop to watch the smallest packages as they kick their little legs in the air, almost losing their balance and falling down. I would love to take a video of them, but they might just kick my ass with those little legs of theirs.

I continue heading — hopefully — toward town, but start to feel a bit uncomfortable as I approach a house with multiple young men outside smoking and drinking beer. I remember what Jon told me on the plane about staying aware of my surroundings, and realize I should've asked him what to do in a

164

situation like this. I tighten the grip on the knife in my pants pocket.

Does 911 even exist in this country? Little late for that now. I make eye contact and say, "Hola," as I briskly walk past. They ignore me and don't return the greeting.

Humph. In past decades, I used to get whistles and obscene comments thrown my way when walking by a group of guys.

Make up your mind, woman. Do you want their attention or not?

No, no. Not interested. Just bitching.

I catch a whiff of something. I sniff the air like a Bassett Hound and realize just how hungry I am. I begin looking around for a soda to catch lunch — and a can of soda!

Further down the road I come across a Chinese restaurant. The smells emanating from within the walls are magnificent and my mouth begins to water. The aroma of meats stir-fried in a wok possibly with vegetables, rice, egg, and a dash of soy sauce tempt my imagination.

This could be my best discovery yet.

As with most of the businesses here in Atenas, the front walls are all open with bistro seating on the sidewalk out front. I go inside to the restaurant and look at the menu. It's in Spanish. My time living in Miami for so many years taught me a few Spanish items on the list, but the Chinese flair to the words is throwing me off. I pull out my dictionary and phone app — *hey, I've got Wi-Fi* — and start translating. Seeing my struggle, the chef, who is Chinese, begins speaking to me in Spanish. It takes my brain a second to adjust. Even though it makes perfect sense, my mind goes, "tilt." If he had opened his mouth and suddenly began speaking Gaelic, I couldn't be more surprised. Not that he *shouldn't* speak Gaelic, but that it would just seem odd to me.

I wonder if he has an interesting name that doesn't fit this picture, like "Harold" or "Sven."

I meet his conversation with the deer in the headlight look and open my mouth to order, but nothing comes out. We stare at each other before I stammer out, "pollo."

The light bulb of understanding comes on in his face that is followed by a string of words I can't keep up with. I think to use my app but remember it won't work without a signal then quickly flip over to my little dictionary.

The chef heaves a sigh, said something in Spanish, and then waves to get my attention. He has gotten a brilliant idea. He begins showing me assorted vegetables and ingredients to which I either shake my head from side to side to indicate "no," or bob my head up and down for the affirmative. We both sigh as he sets about cooking my lunch.

My phone has a signal!

Quickly I fumble to find Jon's home number and punch the buttons. It begins to ring. Big droplets of sweat run down the crack of my ass. I hate that.

"Hola," the voice of an older woman answers.

"Esta Jon ahi?" I stumble through asking for Jon. I think.

"Jon no esta aqui."

"Oh, ummm, ah, tell him Teresa called."

"Que?" She doesn't understand.

I fumble with my Spanish handbook saying, "Uno momento" repeatedly until I put together what I thought was the correct phrase.

"Dile que Teresa llamo," I stop short of leaving my phone number. I don't think either of us can handle that dialogue right now.

"Okay." Probably the only English word she knows. She hangs up.

You're forgetting your epiphany. You don't need a man to be all right.

I don't feel desperate for Jon's attention, as if my trip will be incomplete and ruined if I don't see him again. I can take him or leave him.

Take him! Take him!

It's this intoxicating desire to see him again that would be like the cherry on top of this delectable trip.

That's not the same as the disease of co-dependency, right?

I don't *need* Jon to be acceptable and whole, but I'm not dead yet!

This turbidity of the heart, this dichotomy of chastity and lust, to have yet have not, leaves me off balance like a newborn giraffe, gawky and unstable, but with an innate sense of moving towards the purpose of standing on my own two feet.

The first year following the divorce, I became a non-sexual being. Sex was the furthest thing from my existence. But then it hit me like a hurricane. I needed to be touched. Held. Intimacy became an addiction I had to fight with all my might. I confided in one friend whose understanding comment will stay with me forever.

"Are you Italian?"

"Yes," I answered.

"Well, why didn't you tell me that to begin with? That's the problem right there. It's the nature of Italians to be horny!"

I can't say that her assessment was without merit, but I couldn't help but wonder why my German side wasn't keeping the Italian side in check. I did appreciate her not exploding me with righteous condemnation. The biblical teachings are crystal clear, but the desire was uncontrollable.

Other people engage in meaningless sex to get their jollies and not get emotionally involved. Men do it. I can too.

But I was wrong. My forays into uncommitted sex simply didn't work for me, and I was left feeling frustrated and humiliated. I kept getting ghosted. I assumed because I became smothering and clingy, trying to turn simple sex into a relationship. My heart was in agreement with Gil Grissom from CSI that "sex should provide the opportunity for human connection…sex without love is pointless. It makes you sad." But the war with my body went unchecked.

My Spanish/Chinese meal arrives at the table. The aroma hangs in the air and you can almost taste it. The chicken is moist and flavorful and the vegetables are cooked to just the right level of tenderness.

The chef watches me gobble down mouthfuls of his creation with a smile of satisfaction crossing his face. I give him a thumb's up, which I'm hoping is truly a universal sign of, "good job, bro" and not an obscene gesture.

I've heard that some gestures in America can be misconstrued as offensive in other countries. Making a circle with your thumb and index finger is how to signal "OK" in the U.S., but the same gesture in Brazil is the equivalent of flipping someone the middle finger, while in the Middle East, a thumb's up gesture has the connotation of "up yours!" Thank God I'm not in the Middle East. Between hand gestures and hijabs, I would have an appointment with a machete.

After stuffing my face with the delicious concoction, I get up to pay.

Here we go. Math again. I look at the chef with pleading eyes and hold out all the colones in my possession.

Be gentle with me.

He takes what he deems suitable out of the bundle in my hand. Whatever the amount, it's a fair exchange for a meal so scrumptious.

168

Showing him that I'm not a complete loss at Spanish, I break into my *"Donde esta le parade de taxi"* line. He walks me to the sidewalk and points directions a block or two further down the road then turn left and hands me a fortune cookie.

"Gracias," I say and walk fat and happy to my destination around the corner.

As if ordered for me, a taxi sits there waiting. He quickly hails me over to his car and opens the door.

"A dónde vas?" the driver asks.

"B & B Vista Atenas Hotel"

Fastening my seat belt, we cut and turn our way along the streets back to the hotel. I open my fortune cookie as we ride. The little strip of paper inside says:

"Love is as necessary to human beings as food and shelter."

My feelings exactly.

Take that, Aristotle.

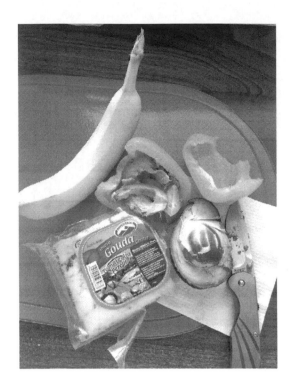

Lunch from the
grocery store

View from
the pool

EL TOLEDO COFFEE FARM

I'm last to arrive for the tour of the coffee farm, and my fellow tourists appear to be composed mainly of one family. All blonde and pale with identical faces.

Geez, if you threw some sugar on 'em, they'd look like freshly-baked sugar cookies.

We introduce ourselves. Gabriel Calderon, the owner and master farmer, leads us out into a seven-acre farm that looks like nothing more than a forest.

Didn't Winnie the Pooh live in the seven-acre wood?

Gabriel is of average height, but is quickly dwarfed by the tall trees. He has a quiet spirit about him and friendly eyes looking out from under the edge of a khaki "Gilligan" style hat. His faded blue cargo pants show the wear of hard work by the frayed edges on the bottoms. His red T-shirt bears a crackled and disappearing white logo, and a leather sheath is slung low around his hips.

"This land has been in our family for many generations, but only within the past few years has it been certified completely organic," says Gabriel.

"How many farms in Costa Rica are organic?" asks one of the sugar cookies who looks to be around nine or ten years old.

"The El Toledo Coffee Farm is one of the less than 1% of coffee farms that practice organic agriculture in Costa Rica," Gabriel answers as he leads us through the forest.

"Did the flavor of the coffee improve when you went organic?" another cookie asks.

"I'll let you be the judge of that later," said Gabriel.

We continue into the forest.

I notice a couple of the six cookie-cutter kids taking notes while others ask excellent questions and the rest are attentive.

After watching them for a while, I ask their mother, "Are you homeschoolers?"

"Ah, yes, yes we are," she says with her nose crinkled up in amazement. "How did you know?"

"Because I homeschooled my three children for eight years," I say, "and I recognize the signs: eager young minds processing information, taking notes, and being interactive with adults."

"What a small world," she says with a big smile. "How old are your children?"

"They're all grown now and in their early thirties. But I have to say, they're pretty amazing people." I puff out my chest. "So, are you and your family in Costa Rica on vacation or here for business?"

"Neither, really," began the trim petite mother of six.

Six kids and she still looks like a model. Damn her thighs.

"See, we are part of the mission trip to help out with the daycare here at the farm."

"A daycare?" I ask.

What next? A petting zoo?

"When it's time for the coffee beans to be harvested," she said, "migrant workers from Nicaragua come here bringing their families, including many small children. The children used to go into the fields with the parents, but that's a very dangerous situation."

"I'm sure," I say looking down around me and assessing what trouble a toddler could get into.

"The Calderon family opened a daycare to watch over and teach the children while keeping them safe. It's run entirely by volunteers and donations."

"That's awesome," I say.

"We felt it would be an excellent experience for our

172

children to learn to serve others and see a new country at the same time. We like to have a balance between academics and hands-on experiences."

"So how long will you be here?" I ask.

"We've signed up to help for a month," she answers.

"A month?" the answer stopping me in my tracks. "Wow! I wish I had had an opportunity like this when I was teaching my kids!" A pang of nostalgia gripped my heart for those years. "We did field trips to the Keys and to The Space Center, but never out of the U.S. Your husband must have a great boss to let him take a month-long mission trip."

"He's the minister at our church, so, yeah, he's got a great boss." She chuckles. "The church subsidizes a portion of the trip, most of our needs are covered by the host country, and we're frugal about our expenses."

The procession comes to a halt and Gabriel loudly clears his throat.

Maybe he's thirsty.

"My kids speak several languages due to our travels," she says as we start walking again. "I'd be lost without their abilities to communicate. I'm not so quick to pick up languages."

"Me neither," I say.

Gabriel stops walking, reaches up and picks an orange off a tree.

"Many years ago," Gabriel says while peeling the orange. "Coffee was grown alone in the fields using synthetic pesticides, herbicides, fungicides, and fertilizers. But after my grandfather developed neurological and intestinal problems from working with chemicals, we had to find another solution." He handed segments of orange out to us.

"How do you know all this stuff?" asks one of the boy cookies. He looks to be around twelve or thirteen.

173

"I attended university in Michigan and earned degrees in chemistry and agriculture for use in converting the plantation over to a more natural, balanced method," he says.

"Is that called permaculture farming?" asks one of the older girl cookies.

"Yes, that's right," replies Gabriel.

"Excuse me, but I'm not as smart as these guys," I say motioning toward the children. "Can you explain more about that for me?"

"Of course," says Gabriel. Permaculture farming involves growing other plants in harmony with the coffee that provide shade for the coffee plants, enriches the soil, and repels pests. So, we grow a variety of trees, fruits, and nuts—that's a cashew tree behind you—along with the coffee plants, influencing temperature and enhancing the flavor of the beans. It's nature in balance.

"This isn't a simple task, as there are lots of hoops to jump through and red tape involved in getting certified organic." He peels another orange and passes it around.

"In the early 1990s, organic certification companies from Europe and the U.S. convinced Costa Rica's coffee farmers to go organic with the offer of a 30% to 50% mark-up, and 'all you have to do is not use chemicals for three years.' They neglected to tell the farmers *how* to do this, and 80% of the coffee farms' plants died."

So much for balance.

Gabriel walks a few more feet and pulls bananas from a tree. Reaching into the leather sheath around his waist, he pulls out a sizeable machete and slices open the bananas, offering pieces to each of us. The cookie cutter boys' eyes widened at the sight.

I turned to the mom of the children again, "I'm sorry, but

I didn't ask your name."

"Gayle. My name's Gayle, and this is my husband Tom." The children had swarmed around Gabriel buzzing with excitement over the machete.

"Pleased to meet you," I say shaking hands with her tall thin husband. "You have a beautiful family and a great boss." The comment took Tom back a second before he caught on and chuckled.

"Oh, yeah," he said. "Excuse me, but I want to go ask Gabriel something," and off he walked.

"With all this farming talk, I can't help but remember our attempt to start a garden in our backyard in Miami," I say to Gayle. "I got a book on small area gardening and let the kids plot out the area on graph paper, indicating where each plant should be placed. I had them read about flowers that if planted around the perimeter of the vegetables, would help to protect against bugs. We ripped out the grass and churned up the soil and used the hoe to form rows. The seeds were delicately placed in the soil at just the right depth and watered to perfection just like the book said. Everything sprouted and grew to beautiful height. There was just one thing wrong. When it came time to harvest the fruits of our labor, every single vegetable came out in miniature form."

Gabriel clears his throat again. I heard it, but I was too deep in conversation to heed his warning.

"Had you planted small versions by mistake?" Gayle asks.

"Nope, I had planted in Ohio soil in my mind when there was Miami sand in my yard. At least that's part of what the Agriculture extension agent hypothesized. That and something about nematodes and using fertilizer."

"'Nematodes,' I asked the extension agent. 'Are those any relation to Bufo Toads, 'cos Miami has plenty of them!'"

"What's a Bufo toad," Gayle laughs.

"It's a humongous poisonous demon toad that won't die! I was introduced to them when a friend's dog grabbed one and began foaming at the mouth. My friend, Barry, grabbed the garden hose, shoved it into the dog's mouth to rinse out the poison, and then smacked the toad with several blows from a shovel. It lay there flattened and motionless."

"Eeeewww," Gayle gurgled, curling her lips with disgust.

"After seeing to the dog again, Barry dug a deep hole and buried the toad. A bit later while grilling steaks for dinner on the back patio, the soil began to stir over where the toad had been buried. Soon, its massive toady toes appeared above ground and it slowly crept out of the grave like a zombie apocalypse!"

"Aaahhhh! How do you kill these things?" Gayle says with her hand to her throat.

"You have to cut them in half!"

"Ahem!" We look over at Gabriel. He and everyone else are staring at us.

With our shoulders bowed and our hands clasped in front of us, we whimpered, "Sorry."

"Does anyone have any questions?" Gabriel asks. "If not, then let's turn around and walk back the way we came and I'll show you the next step in the coffee process."

Everyone does an about face and begins walking toward the tiki hut where we started the tour. Gabriel stops us partway there at a rackety piece of machinery painted green, red, and yellow with gears and bars and something that looks like a hamster wheel.

"This machine separates the coffee bean from the fruit. The picked fruit goes in the top here." Gabriel dumps a basket of freshly picked coffee fruit into a funnel-shaped wood and red metal opening on the top of the machine and turns the antique monstrosity on. The thing comes alive.

176

Gabriel raises his voice over the machinery, "The fruit is being ground away from the bean, here." He points to turning gears and whatchamacallits reaching up and pulling down doohickeys that spin other thingamabobs.

This looks like something out of Willie Wonka's chocolate factory. Any minute now, Oompa Loompas are gonna come running out of the forest.

"As you see, the ground up fruit comes down this trough and drops into this barrel and the beans come out over there and drop into that basket," Gabriel picks up a handful of ground up fruit. "The fruit is either returned back to the soil to fertilize the coffee plants or is fermented and turned into coffee flavored wine."

I'll take a sample of that!

Gabriel turns us around to show us a long black plastic tarp lying on the ground where the beans have been spread out to dry in the sun.

"And here is where we dry the beans before roasting."

A chicken crosses the beans.

Hey, he had to get to the other side! Ba-dum-bump ching!

"Umm, don't the beans get dirty laying there?" Gale's husband, Tom, asks with his left upper lip curled up at the sight of the chicken walking on the beans.

Chicken-foot flavored coffee. Sign me up.

I nudge Gale with my shoulder and say, "Remind me to tell you about a new way to cook chicken." She gives me a curious look.

"The beans get washed before the next step which is roasting, but it's at such a high heat that it destroys any bacteria," Gabriel says.

That's a comforting thought as a few more chickens cross the tarp.

177

Walking further toward the tiki hut, Gabriel stops to show us the roasting of the beans being done in another antique-looking piece of equipment blackened with use. It sort of resembled a small furnace or a smoker.

"This is our artisan coffee roaster, Carlito" Gabriel says as Carlito flashes a wide grin and waves to us. He is a very thin man with mocha-colored skin and closely shaved hair. "Carlito will carefully remove a sample of the beans and look for just the right color for mild, medium, or dark roast coffee."

Good God, it's hot standing next to this roaster. No wonder Carlito is so skinny. All the fat has melted off his body.

Carlito pulls out coffee beans using a u-shaped scoop with a really long handle. The beans glisten in the light against the black handle. He pushes the scoop back into the machine and waits as Gabriel says, "The difference between medium and dark roast can be merely a few seconds. It's a very delicate balance"

Carlito checks the roast again. Darker this time, but apparently not what he's looking for since he reinserts the rod and waits.

"Rather than mechanize our processing of the beans, we choose to maintain our tried-and-true methods of cultivating and roasting coffee by hand, which has served us for so many years, trusting in the natural balance provided by nature."

"Have a seat at the picnic tables," Gabriel says motioning towards the tiki hut. "We're going to play a coffee game. The prize is you get to taste some delicious coffee." He smiles and introduces us to a woman next to a table with cups. "This is Vanessa and she's going to put cups of coffee in front of you, and you're going to tell me which is mild, medium, or dark roast."

I watch the young, petite dark-haired woman as she goes about making coffee in the most rudimentary coffee pots I've ever seen. Basically tri-pods of wood, not unlike milking stools, but with a large hole cut out of the top. Freshly ground coffee is placed inside a cheesecloth "sock" that hangs down through the hole from a strainer-looking thingy. Vanessa pours boiling water through the sock and over the beans until the pitcher below fills up with dripping coffee. This process is repeated two more times as three cups of coffee are lined up in front of each of us.

"Taste each cup and tell me which roast it is," Gabriel says.

I sample one cup and then another. I fail miserably. I definitely don't have the palate to be a professional coffee tester.

Where's the wine?

Gabriel walks around the tables asking us to identify the roast in each of the three cups. Everyone makes their guess. Then he comes to me.

"I can't tell the difference in any of them," I said sheepishly.

"How do you normally take your coffee," Gabriel asks me.

"Cream and Splenda."

"The reason for your failure is because you're not used to tasting the coffee without drowning it in cream or sweetener," his enthusiasm peaking. "You can't taste the flavor of the coffee that way."

"Oh, that's a no-brainer," said one of the women in her late fifties. "I know coffee like the back of my hand."

Arrogant bitch.

Perhaps she would have been right if the coffee had been in clear glass. Simply look through the glass and see how dark it is. However, we can't see the depth of the color of the coffee since they all look the same in the opaque white cups. "But, I don't like dark coffee," interrupted the arrogant woman.

"Which of the three cups did you prefer?" Gabriel says to her.

"This one here in the middle," she replied.

"That is actually the dark roast in the middle cup," Gabriel says.

"Do you remember watching the roasting of the beans?" Gabriel asks us. "That shiny substance covering the beans was not water. That's the acid coming out of the bean as it is roasted," he said. "If you have stomach problems after drinking coffee, you should drink a darker roast since more acid gets roasted out of the bean."

I recall Carlito meticulously watching over the roasting process. So, not only did he watch for the color of the beans to change, but also for the amount of acid roasting out of them. All being carefully balanced in the hands of a skilled artisan.

"Now taste the middle coffee again and see if you can pick out any of the flavors of other plants I showed you while we were walking in the field," Gabriel challenges. I failed at this test, too, although several of the others said they could taste flavors of the fruits on the farm, but I think they were just gunning for more free coffee.

With the tour completed, we had the opportunity to purchase bags of coffee and the primitive coffeemaker pot while posing for photos with Gabriel and the staff.

I start to walk away from the group when I hear Gayle's voice.

"Hey, wait!" Gayle hails me. "You promised to give me a new chicken recipe."

"Oh, yeah, but it's not so much a recipe as much as it is a method of cooking," I say. "I collect funky chicken stuff for my kitchen. I have chickens disguised as cheetahs and zebras, and I have a two-foot square yellow metal 'yield' sign with pictures of chickens on it that says 'Chicken Crossing.' So, when I moved to an apartment with a smaller kitchen, some of the chickens had to go. However, I kept the metal yield sign and hung it on the wall behind my stove."

"Many a chicken have crossed over that stove," Gayle giggled.

"Exactly! Great place for the sign, right? One day, I pulled the stove out away from the wall to retrieve a pot holder which had fallen behind there. As luck would have it, I hit the metal sign with my broom as I was retrieving the potholder. The sign slipped from the nail on which it was hanging and fell down exactly into the sliver of space between the plug and the socket, and the metal sign came in contact with the prongs of the plug. ZZZZZAP! Sparks and flames shot out and the smell of metal melting filled the air. The chicken sign fell over onto the floor, smoking. With the potholder, I picked up what was left of the scorched sign. There was a circular shape matching the socket missing from the metal that had 'cooked' away a large portion of the chicken pictures painted on its front. You know, I've roasted chicken, boiled chicken, braised chicken, and baked chicken, but that's the first time I've ever electrocuted chicken!"

Gayle laughed and gave me a little push on the arm as we said our goodbyes.

I purchase bags of coffee to smuggle back into the United States, but since I can't be certain of getting the coffee-flavored wine back, I pass on buying it.

However, the best gift I leave El Toledo Coffee Farm with is the feeling of being part of something fabulous and the balanced life they lead. Work. Family. Community. It has become apparent to me just how out of balance my life was before this trip.

I was growing old not just from the number of years I'd lived, but I was growing old from abandoning my ideals. I'd given up my passion for life. I read somewhere that years may

181

wrinkle the skin with crow's feet and laugh lines, but to give up enthusiasm wrinkles the soul.

Now, though, I am rejuvenated like lotion to dry elbows through the salve that is Costa Rica.

Roasting coffee   Drying beans

Gabriel

I return to B & B Vista Atenas and see Vera waiting for me.

"Vera! I can't thank you enough for arranging that tour for me," I say.

"You liked?" She grins widely.

"I loved it!"

"I'm so happy I could find something you enjoyed so much," Vera says, giddy as a teenager. "I want to hear all about it. Come. I fix you a plate of dinner. You eat and we talk."

Dinner was…scrambled eggs, salad with the now infamous Lizano sauce and white rice and black beans. Life here is as it should be.

Being talked out and the daylight waning, I climb into bed with a full heart and a slight tugging at its strings to throw caution to the wind and start a new life here in Costa Rica. Vera did it, but that's not my reality.

Screw reality.

It's time to be filled with *pura vida*. I lie in bed, and look to a few clouds moving slowly across the sky. The cool glow of the moon outlining the clouds in silver. I cast shadows on the wall with my hands, my mind fixed on the silver lining of what the future may hold for me. I think of Jon and I regret that I didn't get to see him before leaving Costa Rica. I see him white-water rafting then zip lining with me, his muscular arms catching me as I fly onto the platform, toes pointed in a graceful ballet attitude, overlooking the vibrant green of the rainforest.

Oh, who am I kidding? I'm just sorry I didn't get to look into those gorgeous eyes of his and have my way with him!

"Ladies and gentlemen, we've been given clearance to land at the Fort Lauderdale airport," the captain announces over the intercom. "Please place your seats in their full upright positions, store any items you may have removed during the flight, and make sure your seatbelt is securely fastened across your lap. We will be landing shortly."

I wonder how many times he's said that in his life.

The sound of seat belts clicking and stashing of items back into overhead compartments fills the plane.

The flight attendants have assisted in cleaning up the stinky man as best as possible and he is back in his seat. My things were brought to my new seat in the rear of the plane so I would not have to be subjected to the unsavory situation at my previous perch.

The plane touches down onto U.S. soil, and my adventure is over. I'm not sad, though, that it has come to an end because I know the experience will stay with me forever, and I am changed. I can return to my dull, ordinary life with a new attitude (not the ballet movement of the Chicago woman from the raft) knowing that there is more waiting to be explored, both in the world and inside of me.

Yes, I'm sixty years old. I can't change that, but I can change how I live my daily life for the next twenty years. I can make choices to bring more vitality into my existence. I can challenge myself each day to live with purpose and make sure each hour counts for something. I can withhold instant judgments of people based upon appearances and thereby make new friends. I don't have to restrict myself to the rocking chair of indecision, not traveling to exciting places because of the fear of going solo.

As I wait in the aisle to deplane, I wonder, will I come back? What had I missed, besides Jon, which would entice me to make a return visit?

Ahhhh, the space around me is shrinking and I'm starting to sweat. Don't panic. Think. What didn't you get to do?

Umm, there was the Sloth Sanctuary and its local star, Buttercup, not far from Limon where Jon had said wasn't so safe. You can't hold the sloths for the reasons I learned earlier in the trip, but you get to observe more about these little-known animals and see the ongoing research and caregiving they require.

Note to self: Buy a stuffed sloth. Ugh, we're still not moving. Take your mind off it.

I would love to explore San Jose or Sarchi located northwest of the capital. Sarchi is famous for its painted oxcarts. In the 19th century while Americans were arguing with women over the right to vote while wearing dead birds on their heads, farmers in Costa Rica struggled to make a meager living looking for a way to transport their coffee from the mountains to the port. They started using painted oxen carts, which has become Costa Rica's national symbol. I'm not sure where I would put such a thing in a fifth-floor, two-room apartment, but maybe they have itty-bitty tiny ones for sale.

Oh, and I didn't get to experience the blue water of the Rio Celeste in Tenorio Volcano National Park. Two clear rivers feed into one river, but when they mix together to form the Rio Celeste, elements of minerals in both rivers cause the ph level to drop and the suspended particles turn a glorious turquoise color. I want to swim in that water until my fingers and toes turn all pruney.

My God, what is taking so long to get off this plane? Claustrophobia here, people!

I sink into thought of the last evening in Costa Rica at the B & B Vista Atenas Hotel. That night the light was so bright, I couldn't sleep. I left my room and went out to the pool area overlooking the city. The full moon appeared to be so close that you felt like it was going to roll right over the town and squish it.

I sat by the pool looking out over the city of Atenas. The trees below blew in the breeze intermittently blocking the illumination from the city lights, twinkling out a kind of Morse Code that said, "Come back soon."

ENOUGH IS ENOUGH

WhatsApp? Who would be calling me through WhatsApp? The only time I used that was when I was in Costa Rica.

"Hello?" I answer.

"Hello, I miss you," he says. It's Jon.

OMG! Every muscle in my body seizes up and my fingers begin tingling. I didn't know if I was going to orgasm or pass out.

"Jon! I-I'm so surprised to hear from you," I say tripping over my tongue as it dragged on the floor. "I tried calling you several times in Costa Rica. We never got to have dinner."

"My phone. It was broken," he reminds me.

True, it had been difficult to see his photos on the plane because of the cracked screen.

"Broken not just the screen, but inside. I had to get money to buy new one."

"I'm happy you got a new phone and even more excited that you saved my number," I say.

"How was your flight back home?" Jon asks in his honey-like voice.

"What a nightmare!" I tell him about the mess with the stinky old man adding, "The trip was lonely without you to keep me company." I pull out my most sultry voice.

"Oh, baby, I would have been there with you if I could have," he sighs.

Spread me on toast 'cos I just turned to butter and melted.

Trying to regain my composure, I say, "May I ask you something that's been on my mind ever since we landed in Costa Rica? Why couldn't you go through the x-ray machine in the airport?"

Jon lets out a roguish laugh. "Well, umm...see...umm, I have metal on my body."

"Yes, I saw them in your ears and your eyebrow. Why would those have stopped you from going through the x-ray machine?"

"Umm, I have more in other places. Places under my clothes you didn't see."

"Oh!"

I'm not sure what to think about this. I've not encountered one *there* before. Normally, I don't care for tattoos or piercings, but on him somehow they're attractive.

So, I say what any red-blooded American female would say. "Send me a picture."

"You send me picture, too."

His photos come through. Whoa.

This guy has more punctures than a barefoot tourist walking through a bed of spiny sea urchins.

"Now you," he said.

One picture turned into several, with increasing degrees of seduction. Then videos passed between us, shamefully explicit. Like a greyhound chasing a mechanical rabbit around a track, I allow him to lead me down that same course of desperation I had always run before, all the while silently suspecting I may never catch the enticement.

Months pass staying in contact this way before I receive a text from him that simply reads, "I come to U.S. on June 11."

OH, MY, GOD, squeals my inner teenage self. Logic and Reason poke up their heads reminding me of Jon's age, but the idea of being with him is overruling all rational thinking.

You're enough, remember? What about your mountaintop epiphany? I elbow the voices into a windowless room of my mind and shove an imaginary chair under the doorknob.

"Who is picking you up at the airport?" I text while a thousand questions swirl around inside my head. Where will he

190

stay? Does he have money? Is he looking for a job? But a thought creeps in. Is he just using me to gain citizenship? I shove that thought quickly over of the cliff of desire into the dark abyss of denial.

In broken English, a text comes back, "Yes, she gets me. Thank you."

SHE? Well, there it is, someone else is picking him up, taking him out on the town, taking him into her home. With hot jealousy, I erase his messages, but stop short of "un-friending" him on Facebook. I slam down my phone—as hard as you would expect to slam down something that costs around $700.00—and pretend I don't care.

But that's a lie. I had an incredible attraction to this man on the plane to Costa Rica. I loved the feelings of being attractive and desirable again that he released in me. I *craved* it like some addict desperate for cocaine.

I pick my phone back up, making sure the screen isn't broken, and try the communication with Jon again, this time translating my message into Spanish first.

Now, it is clear: he wants me to pick him up at the airport.

The hyperventilating starts up again, and my mind is swirling with plans. The plane would be coming in late on a Friday night. I checked into reserving a hotel room by the airport. Jon said he wanted to look for a job right away, and I reasoned his best bet for functioning with limited English would be to take him to Hialeah where Spanish prevails. He will be flying into Fort Lauderdale International Airport, which is already *halfway* to Hialeah, so it makes no sense to take him back north to my apartment. That's what I reasoned, anyway.

I have it all planned out—people to help him find a place to live and people to help him find a job. I am doing what I do best—planning out someone else's life, not mine.

The day arrives to head to the airport. I know the arrival time. Since Jon would have to go through customs, I decide to look for him by the International Flights exit.

It's a hoax, I tell you! He's playing you.

Ooo, I hope he plays with me. I visualize a guitar being slammed over the head of my voice of reason like in an old cartoon, *"El Kabong"* trying to knock some sense back into my head. But just as in cartoons, it doesn't deter the character from her mission.

I slowly circle the airport expecting to see Jon emerge at any minute from International Flights.

I wait. And circle. And wait and circle some more. Two hours go by and still I hear nothing. I swallow the truth that threatens to well up into my throat like vomit.

Could I have missed him somehow?

Yeah, right, like you'd miss an elephant sitting on the sidewalk getting a pedicure!

I park, get out of the car, and enter the terminal. I relentlessly walk the entire airport looking for Jon, but he is nowhere to be found. Was his plane delayed? I check the flights coming in from Costa Rica. All on time.

I text. I call. Nothing. The clock is ticking on toward the three-hour mark and my anticipation gives way to anger.

I've been duped.

I stomp back to the car, hot tears streaming down my face. I sit with the car in park through the waterworks. Muscles quivering with rage, I pound my fists on the steering wheel for being so gullible and stupid.

What happened to your rainforest "epiphany?"

The crying ultimately subsides and I start the car. I drive north on I-95 hurtling wildly toward home, screaming in psychotic mortification for once again falling prey to my elementary need for affirmation.

He's probably laughing his ass off right now.

The day my adventure to Costa Rica began and I first set eyes on Jon in the airport, I immediately thought he was a terrorist. Now I'm sure of it. He's a terrorist of the heart.

Once home, I sink into despair and disgrace. It is now as it has always been my stumbling block—wanting to be adored by a man and throwing all caution to the proverbial wind while ignoring the red flags waving in my head.

Without fail, every relationship of mine that ended on a bad note came with prior warning flags. All of them exhibited behaviors that I dismissed as things to which I could "adjust."

So, I turned a blind eye to the warning signs in spite of that gut feeling gnawing at me beneath the surface. With each inevitable failure, the emotional state of inadequacy would drive my self-worth further into the ground, leaving me to accept men who couldn't fill the emptiness I held inside.

I find myself right back in that hole described in *There's a Hole in My Sidewalk: The Romance of Self-Discovery* that I keep falling into in spite of the fact that I KNOW it's there.

Jon ghosted me. Ghosting has been such a large part of my life that I've come to expect it.

Practically every summer growing up, my father would take us camping in the Upper Peninsula of Michigan where my mother's relatives lived. I was only a child, but when I met my fourth cousin, Barry, a couple of years older than I, we were instantly drawn to each other and became the best of friends. Looking back on it, I think it was love in its purest form.

The years passed and we grew closer with time. One summer after I turned fifteen, we knew it was more than just friendship. We held hands, he put his arm around me, and we talked for hours, but he never kissed me. I still have the letter

193

professing his love saying he was coming to see me in two weeks.

That letter was the last I ever heard from him. I called every relative in Michigan looking for information when he didn't show up. No one would tell me anything. They said they didn't know where he was.

Then one day as I walked home from school, I saw a car in my family's driveway. The tag read, "Michigan."

My heart pounded in my chest with excitement. He's here! I dropped my textbooks on the sidewalk and ran into the house, bursting through the door shouting his name.

"Barry! Barry!—Hi, Aunt Shirley—Barry," I shout out running past my aunt and my mother at the kitchen table. "Where is he? I can't believe he's finally here! Where are you, Barry?" I raced through the house searching in every spot I could imagine then apprehensively slinked back to the kitchen, a sinking feeling settling into my stomach.

"Teresa, sit down," my Aunt said tapping the table by the chair next to her.

"Barry didn't come with you, did he?" I whispered, afraid that if I spoke it out loud, it would make it real.

"No. He won't be coming."

Tears welled up in my eyes, and I said in disbelief, "No, no, he said he was coming to see me. I have his letter."

"Teresa, you don't know the real Barry. He's not the kind of person you need to be involved with. He left Michigan and moved to Tennessee. He's shacked up with some whore in a trailer there. He likes to live fast and loose. You're not the type of girl he's looking for. You're just not *enough* for him." The words cut through my gut like a sword, slicing me in half.

I'm not enough? What's that mean? I'm not what? Am I not interesting enough? Not smart enough? Not pretty enough? Not slutty enough?

194

That's the moment when the lie was sewn. I'm not enough.

Now, decades later, I'm curled up in a ball on my bed experiencing the same rejection. Darkness surrounds me as I relive every ghosting experience throughout my life. Heaviness pulls me under like a cinder block tied to my ankle. Sinking, I claw at the disappearing light, but it squishes out through my clinched fists and gets eaten by the blackness.

If only… I should have… I could have… all shoot through my brain, arrows of regret piercing my confidence. *Get up and fight!* I scream inside my head, but only emptiness and condemnation are there to meet me. Defeat walls me in on every front, my strength drains as I navigate for the escape, but collapse into the heap of hopes gone awry.

Sleep it off. Don't think anymore. Sleep, I tell myself as I drift off.

I wait by the international customs exit. He comes around the corner. Sea-glass green eyes glistening when he sees me. The bags drop to the floor as he throws his arms around me in a huge bear hug. My nose catches his scent and takes me back to the Costa Rican rainforest.

"Baby, you are here," he says in my ear.

"Where else could I be?"

He pulls back slightly and I can tell he is leaning in to kiss me, but I hold him off with my hands.

"Not yet," I say. "Our kiss will be fiery. I want it to be someplace special. Not here."

The lock to the hotel room opens with a loud buzz to reveal the luxurious king-size bed. We drop our bags. Jon says, "I take a quick shower," and disappears into the bathroom. I adjust the AC colder and begin to remove my shirt when Jon pokes his head out from the bathroom door.

*"Don't take off your clothes. I want to do that," he says
and closes the door.*

*Anticipation of what's to happen grows as I turn down
the bedcovers. Jon emerges from the bathroom wearing a towel
slung low around his hips. I run to turn off the lights in the
room, but he stops me.*

"No. I want to see your face when I bring you pleasure."

*An icy hot chill runs through my body. Pleasure. The
word itself exudes a physical response. His hands cup my face as
he slowly moves in to kiss my lips ever so gently. Again. Again.
I am caught up in time standing still as we savor the mystery of
the simple kiss. I want him.*

*His hands slide down my neck and over my shoulders.
We embrace, arms entwined around each other's bodies. I look
up at him to see he is staring at me with those hypnotic green
eyes of his. He lowers his gaze and takes his time unbuttoning
the top button on my blouse. The second, then the third. As he
opens my shirt, there are no breasts, but a massive gaping hole
all the way through my body. Jon's eyes grow wide and he moves
closer cautiously pushing his hands through the void out to the
other side. His eyes meet mine in an incredulous stare.*

"Teresa," he says and vanishes.

Sucking in a quick breath, my eyes spring open, but I can't
shut off the dream in my head.

I hear it again: *You are enough.*

"I'm *not* enough," I rail against God throwing the glass from
my nightstand against the wall. It splinters into a million shards
like my self-worth. "I will never be free from this foolishness. I'm
doomed to fall prey to this weakness forever. It's an addiction I
can't shake. No one wants me. I'm not enough."

Slumping onto the bed, rational thought seeps in, and I

realize I am approaching the red danger zone of a major depression. I refuse to go deeper into that darkness. So, I shake myself loose of the tentacles of despair holding me down and vow not to stay in this condition. Pulling myself up from the bed, I go in search of the broom.

I sweep away the debris of shattered glass and think of ways to return balance to my insanity.

In *Eat Pray Love*, the author takes a year off to travel three countries in an effort to find herself after a heartbreaking divorce, a tumultuous romance, and debilitating depression. First she immerses herself in the pleasure of living in Italy. Author Elizabeth Gilbert then struggles in India and Indonesia to make major changes in her life and learn how to achieve balance.

Must I travel halfway around the world and sit cross-legged on a tile floor for hours to find balance in my life?

Instead I decide to crawl out of the hole in the sidewalk and go back to square one.

My phone dings. It's Jon.

"I tried entering the US without proper paperwork and was detained in Atlanta," he texts.

The phone rings. It's him.

"They didn't believe I come to US as tourist. They say they think I come to work," he said.

We'd talked about this on the phone before. I'd gotten a crash course in immigration. A tourist visa has limitations and he'd just been in the U.S. Too soon for him to return. He could join the military, but neither of us saw that as an option.

"Or, I could marry a U.S. citizen," he says with a hint in his voice.

DING! DING! DING! And there it is.

My voice of reason clangs the gong long and hard, and strangely enough there are no dissenting voices in my head this time.

I never wanted to admit it, but I think I knew all along his interest came with ulterior motives. I may have shoved this thought out of my head before, but the door is now flung completely open and the red flags are heaped in a pile in full view for me to see. I can no longer ignore the obvious.

His statement is just the right dose of methadone I need to break this addiction.

"I'm sorry," I say, "but that's not an option."

"I thought you liked me. Don't you want me anymore," he pleads.

"Not like this." I end the call and turn off the phone.

There it was, the bitch-slap statement I needed to get my teenage hormones back into submission. I'll have the same reaction to a man asking me for a loan as asking me about getting married. Marriage isn't out of the question, but if it comes my way, it won't be with someone looking for asylum or a handout. My lust carries me only so far.

Balance needs to be restored between my licentious desires and my logic.

The theory of balance has been all around me. Hippocrates in his theory that a person needs to be mentally and physically in balance. Elizabeth Gilbert in *Eat, Pray, Love* seeking balance through her journey of healing. Gabriel preached it on his coffee farm with balance in the soil and the variety of plants so the coffee beans could produce the best flavor. I need to find balance between my gullible nature and my protective measures in order to avoid ridiculous situations like this that wind up hurting my heart, without pushing men away. I need to find balance in order to be complete in who I am so I will stop looking for it in another person.

The epiphany should have been enough to straighten me out, but I failed at achieving this balance. We all fail. We've all fallen short of the platform of perfection and have to be rescued.

You are enough.

The marquee sign of understanding flickers in my brain, then glows brightly. If I'm able to come to God with all my failures, faults, and frustrations and *still* be enough, then He is not just telling me that *I* am enough, but that *He* is enough to bridge the gap between my lustful thoughts and piety. He is enough to sustain me in my loneliness. He is enough to protect me from fear in a garden of snakes lurking overhead, sailing through clouds on a wire, and from losing my mind over the flattery of a young man.

I no longer need to feel old and unwanted or blister my self-esteem with an equal dose of self-flagellation. If I'm enough for the Creator of the universe, then I no longer need to feel unloved.

I have found my Fountain of Youth. Stretching beyond my comfort zone and daring to explore new places, new experiences, and new people opens the gate to life beyond the living room rocking chair. The elixir of youth is living out loud.

No, I shall "not go gentle in to that good night," nor do I have to go slipping into it through the oily sea of sadness. I can choose to go whooping and laughing the whole way — solo, if necessary.

I planned a trip to Costa Rica all on my own, climbed a damn volcano, went white water rafting, and zip lined on my freaking sixtieth birthday and didn't die from a snake bite or break my neck in a fall. I was enough then, and I'm enough now.

Can terrifying thoughts take control, binding me with a 2-ply cord of inadequacy and fear of the future and cause me to stumble? Of course, but it no longer needs to defeat me and send me spiraling down into the abyss of depression. I no longer have to succumb to feelings of dread by being home alone on a Saturday night. Insecurity can only control me if I give it the power to do so. I am free to be me, imperfect, but able to rise above my weaknesses. Fear, loneliness, and desperation may poke their ugly heads up from the crevasses in my brain, but I can pound them back down with the rubber mallet of acceptance like in the arcade game "Whack A Mole." I am acceptable to God just as I am with all of my flaws and shortcomings, worthy to come to Him.

Still, I had fallen in love. I wanted to travel to defy my age, to slow down time and be absorbed so deeply in living that age would become irrelevant. Costa Rica had done that. My fountain of youth bubbled in my hands for eight days. I saw a new place, but more importantly, I had seen it through new eyes—Jon's eyes, those gorgeous sea-glass green eyes that reflected the vibrancy of youth and life in Costa Rica, setting the stage for my transformation.

Though not the romantic adventure I had built up in my imagination, I had fallen in love, just not with a person. I'd fallen for a country.

Travel writer and novelist, Pico Iye sums it up so well. "…every trip to a foreign country can be a love affair, where you're left puzzling over who you are and whom you've fallen in love with."

Did I imagine Jon or was he just a metaphor for my love affair with Costa Rica?

I watch a storm roll in beyond my sunroom, while contemplating my affair. The sky blackens behind the top floor of the apartment buildings across the lake. Leaves fly past my window caught in the updrafts of the wind unable to control their journey.

The first fat drop of rain splats wide against the glass and slips slowly towards the bottom of the window frame. But before it gets there, more raindrops plop hard against the glass and join its path. Soon the view of the world beyond the pane smears into

200

Salvador Dali distorted images. The distortion leaves with the storm's passing washing away dirt and grime from the exterior of the glass. The nascent acceptance of myself finds the cleansing symbolic.

I stride across the room to my laptop, shoulders back, no longer weighed down with a burden of inadequacy. I push the power button on my Mac and it chimes. I click on the web browser.

Online dating website? Hardly.

"My Bucket List" opens up onto the screen. I read through the entries, deleting from the list, "Find a man," and "Drop dress size to single digits."

I click on the boxes in front of three of my goals:

"Go zip lining in Costa Rica."
"Go white water rafting."
"Discover something healing."

My chest rises as I heave a deep sigh of confidence. "With whom shall I fall in love next?"

The End

"You are never too old to set another goal
or to dream a new dream."
—C.S. Lewis

ABOUT THE AUTHOR

As a transplant from Ohio, Teresa came to Miami, Florida, for a visit and found that sand suited her better than snow. She attended Miami-Dade Community College and worked for the public school system for several years until marrying and starting a family. She became a divorcee stay-at-home mom, homes-schooling three children for eight years before heading back to the work force. Teresa has now been employed with a financial advisor firm for eighteen years. With this, her premier book, she is focused on a new chapter of her life sharing her most excellent adventure with the masses. Well, maybe not the masses, but with others looking to make their golden years come alive.

Made in the USA
Monee, IL
05 June 2022

868c2dd3-169d-49c3-a45f-aa5d8874679fR01